Centering Hope as a Sustainable Decolonial Practice

POSTCOLONIAL AND DECOLONIAL STUDIES IN RELIGION AND THEOLOGY

Series Editor
Sheryl Kujawa-Holbrook, Claremont School of Theology

Series Editorial Board

Jon Berquist, Stephen Burns, Cláudio Carvalhaes, Jennifer Te Paa Daniel, Lynne St. Clair Darden, Christine J. Hong, Wonhee Anne Joh, HyeRan Kim-Cragg, Boyung Lee, Aprilfaye Tayag Manalang, Loida Yvette Martell, Stephanie Y. Mitchem, Jea Sophia Oh, Nicolas Esteban Panotto, Jeremy Punt, Patrick Reyes, Joerg Rieger, Fernando Segovia, Melinda McGarrah Sharp, Kay Higuera Smith, Jonathan Y. Tan, Mona West, and Amos Yong.

This series responds to the growing interest in postcolonial studies and re-examines the hegemonic, European-dominated religious systems of the old and new empires. It critically addresses the colonial biases of religions, the academy, and local faith communities, in an effort to make these institutions more polyvocal, receptive, and empowering to global cultures and epistemologies. The series will engage with a variety of hybrid, overlapping, and intersecting definitions of postcolonialism—as a critical discursive practice, as a political and ideological stance concerned with exposing patterns of dominance and hegemony, and as contexts shaped by ongoing colonization and decolonization. Books in the series will also explore the relationship between postcolonial values and religious practice, and the transformation of religious symbols and institutions in postcolonial contexts beyond the academy. The series aims to make high-quality and original research available to the scholarly community. The series welcomes monographs and edited volumes which forge new directions in contextual research across disciplines and explore key contemporary issues. Established scholars as well as new authors will be considered for publication, including scholars "on the margins" whose voices are under-represented in the academy and in religious discourse. Authors working in sub-disciplines of religious studies and/or theology are encouraged to submit proposals.

Recent Titles

Centering Hope as a Sustainable Decolonial Practice: Esperanza en Práctica, by Yara González-Justiniano

Mark and Literary Materialism: A Lesson in Reading Liberation, by Niall McKay

Postcolonial Preaching: Creating a Ripple Effect, by HyeRan Kim-Cragg

Decolonial Futures: Intercultural and Interreligious Intelligence for Theological Education, by Christine Hong

Unmasking White Preaching: Racial Hegemony, Resistance, and Possibilities in Homiletics, edited by Lis Valle-Ruiz and Andrew Wymer

Sámi Nature-centered Christianity in the European Arctic: Indigenous Theology beyond Hierarchical Worldmaking, by Tore Johnsen

Centering Hope as a Sustainable Decolonial Practice

Esperanza en Práctica

Yara González-Justiniano

LEXINGTON BOOKS
Lanham • Boulder • New York • London

Published by Lexington Books
An imprint of The Rowman & Littlefield Publishing Group, Inc.
4501 Forbes Boulevard, Suite 200, Lanham, Maryland 20706
www.rowman.com

86-90 Paul Street, London EC2A 4NE

Copyright © 2022 by The Rowman & Littlefield Publishing Group, Inc.

All rights reserved. No part of this book may be reproduced in any form or by any electronic or mechanical means, including information storage and retrieval systems, without written permission from the publisher, except by a reviewer who may quote passages in a review.

British Library Cataloguing in Publication Information Available

Library of Congress Cataloging-in-Publication Data

Names: González-Justiniano, Yara, author.
Title: Centering hope as a sustainable decolonial practice : esperanza en práctica / Yara González-Justiniano.
Description: Lanham : Lexington Books, [2022] | Series: Postcolonial and decolonial studies in religion and theology | Includes bibliographical references and index.
Identifiers: LCCN 2022029532 (print) | LCCN 2022029533 (ebook) | ISBN 9781793650917 (paper) | ISBN 9781793650894 (cloth) | ISBN 9781793650900 (ebook)
Subjects: LCSH: Christianity--Puerto Rico. | Postcolonial theology--Puerto Rico. | Hope--Religious aspects--Christianity.
Classification: LCC BR645.P7 G65 2022 (print) | LCC BR645.P7 (ebook) | DDC 277.295--dc23/eng/20220725
LC record available at https://lccn.loc.gov/2022029532
LC ebook record available at https://lccn.loc.gov/2022029533

To the love for the things I will never see but abundantly live for.

Contents

Acknowledgments	ix
List of Figures	xv
Chapter One: About Context: "No Hay Mal que Dure Cien Años, Ni Cuerpo que lo Resista."	1
Chapter Two: About Hope: "Al Mal Tiempo, Buena Cara"	21
Chapter Three: About Practice: "A Buen Entendedor, Pocas Palabras Bastan"	43
Chapter Four: About the Future: "Vivir del Cuento"	67
Chapter Five: About Telos: "Más Largo que la Esperanza del Pobre"	101
Notes	117
Bibliography	143
Index	151
About the Author	183

Acknowledgments

When the post office opened in Puerto Rico about two weeks after the Hurricane, I started sending boxes filled with supplies for my family, their neighbors and whomever I could reach. Only people with a Post Office Box could receive mail, so people who had them became the contact for distribution. I called my *madrina,* who miraculously had reception, to let her know about the boxes I had shipped with solar chargers, batteries, water filters, etc. And before hanging up, she said to me "*tu eres nuestra esperanza*" (you are our hope) and then hung up. These words haunt me in a powerful way to this day. I was in a position to serve my family, because others had served me, and enabled me to provide. She, however, was not referring to what it meant for her to wait for the boxes nor putting the burden on my shoulders to fulfil her hopes. She was telling me that I had been their hope since the moment they learned I was on my way into the world. She was referring to the ways I had been raised and nurtured in the hopes that I would be ready to face the daily trials and struggles in solidarity with others. I was their hope because I was moved to be the one they had raised in hope. This work is the birthing of the hope my family, my loved ones, and my faith sowed.

GRACIAS TO MY FAMILY. I begin thanking my family, friends, and accomplices without whom the *ánima* and *ánimo* in this work would not be possible. Those who have watched over me from a distance, this work is ours! *Gracias* to my parents, Miguel González Pérez and Marisol Justiniano Aldebol, for your infinite support, love, and unquivering encouragement. This work is pregnant with your wisdom. You are my inspiration; I am who you raised me to be, *los amo entrañablemente. Gracias* to my *madrina,* Rosa Evelyn Figueroa Sánchez, for raising my political conscience and my love for Puerto Rico, for always speaking her truth and for not letting me forget that I am named after a revolution. Love, *Ayuburí.*

Gracias to my ancestors *abuela* Lumi, *abuela* Otilia, *abuela* Carmen "Monino," Carlos "Willie," and Lydia "Nin." *Gracias* to my *abuela,* Rosalía for the prayers, *pasteles,* and *sofrito* that fed me during crunch time and made me feel closer to home. A special *gracias* to my sister, Tania María, for her artistic contribution on the cover. You are the reason for my unconditional love. *Gracias* to my *tías* and *tíos* who have cheered me on, Maribel, Ángel, Ivys, Vilma, George, José, Jacqueline, Albita, and Jerry; and *primos* Ariana, Andrea, Pablo Andrés, and Ricardo. *Gracias* to my *compadres* Angeliz and Jonathan, for believing in me and supporting my goals even when it meant leaving. *Gracias* to dear Leisa and Amy, for checking up on me, cheering me on, indulging me, and accompanying me. *Gracias* to Patricia and Jesús for walking with me through thick and thin. *Gracias* to my *comadre* Diliana, for her attentive listening and companionship. Especial *gracias* to my *prima* Amanda, who witnessed a year of daily writing, kept me company, and shared with me her sweet charisma. *Gracias* to my *ahijadas, sobrinos,* and *sobrinas*, for being my joy and hope in the process of writing and researching; Lyanna, Lia, Delianis, Xin-Xin, Hugo, Cecilia, and Eliana.

GRACIAS TO ALL OF THOSE WHO SUSTAINED AND SUPPORTED THIS ACADEMIC WORK. *Gracias* to all the congregations and collaborators of this project who welcomed me and shared the practices of hope that enlivened this project: pastors and congregations of Iglesia Cristiana (Discípulos de Cristo) en Fajardo, Iglesia San Francisco de Asís in Old San Juan (Catholic), la Primera Iglesia Bautista de Carolina, Mar Azul (Independent), Iglesia de Dios Misión Internacional de Río Piedras (Pentecostal), and La Travesía (PCA). I am in your debt. *Gracias* to Bryan P. Stone's guidance, perseverance and friendship who has been instrumental for the conception and completion of this work. *Gracias* for asking the question that I have tirelessly worked to answer and for guiding me in its search. *Gracias* to Teresa Delgado, whose passionate work made a way for my work. I am indebted for the opportunity to work and be shaped by the wisdom and passion of her scholarship. I am grateful for her friendship and mentorship in this journey. *Gracias* to the faculty at Boston University School of Theology whose wisdom steered this work; Rady Roldán-Figueroa, and Jonathan Calvillo who took their time to critically engage with my work, who have prayed for me and seen me through. *Gracias* to Cristian De La Rosa, for her support, counseling, and faith in my work through all these years. Like a true teacher, she mirrored my questions and helped me draft the thesis of my work, written on a napkin, that I conserve, over Mexican food. Her commitment to the empowerment of the Latinx community through education inspires me to continue *la lucha*.

Gracias to my colleagues at Vanderbilt Divinity School for their warm welcome and providing a space to become; and especial gratitude to Phillis Isabella Sheppard for her encouragement, support, and patient listening. *Gracias* to my former colleagues at Garrett-Evangelical Theological Seminary for your care, trust, and lifegiving wisdom; I miss you! *Gracias* to my former students at Garrett-Evangelical Theological Seminary and Vanderbilt Divinity School, for testing these ideas with me. *Gracias* to my research assistant Rubén David Bonilla, a brilliant scholar in the making. *Gracias* to the Hispanic Theological Initiative and the Forum for Theological Exploration. I am grateful for these institutions whose dedication to my success in this process became my lifeline. *Gracias* to my HTI and FTE colleagues who made all this work less burdensome through their company and who make me have hope in the academy through their brilliant scholarship; especially Jorge Juan Rodríguez, Aly Benítez, Lydia Hernández, Jasmin Figueroa, and Johana Yunker for checking up on me. *Gracias* to Joanne Rodríguez, HTI director, who gifted me her wisdom and support when I most needed it. *Gracias*, to the spirits of those who witnessed through their work and kindled my work while in the solitude of writing, Rubem Alves, Gloria Anzaldúa, and Patrick Reyes. Patrick, you embody *un espíritu dadivoso y desprendido*. You know what it means to wisely steward and distribute resources to foster the flourishing of others. *Gracias* to my colleagues from Art, Religion, and Culture Collaborative, and colleagues from the Association of Practical Theology, for your intellectual and spiritual nurturing. *Gracias* to my HTI editors Ulrike Guthrie and Catherine Osborne, and Anastasia Kidd for taking the time and energy to walk with me, repeatedly, through my writing. *Gracias* to all the scholars who encouraged me at different stages and believed in me and my work, Agustina Luvis Nuñez, Elizabeth Conde-Frazier, Ediberto López, Nancy Bedford, Mai-Anh Tran, Wanda Stahl, Loida Martell, Luis Rivera Pagán, and Cláudio Carvalhaes.

GRACIAS TO ALL WHO SUSTAINED ME IN BODY, MIND AND SPIRIT. *Gracias* to my dear fierce friends and amazing colleagues, Kathryn House and Xochitl Alvizo, who shared their wisdom, affirmation, and guidance with me throughout this journey; they leave me in awe. *Gracias* for holding on to me and keeping me in the light. You are huge! *Gracias* to my brilliant *cubanas*, Marlene Ferreras and Grace Vargas, my partners in crime. Their friendship, feedback, and sense of humor carried me through. *Gracias* to Julissa Ossorio, Lilian Arroyo, and Yoely Castro for our biannual four-hour-long meals that energized my spirit and affirmed my work. *Gracias*, to my friend Jason Juan Rodríguez, for talking me off the ledge every time I thought I was not going to make it; I can! *Gracias* to my friend Andrew del Pilar, who challenged me at every turn, *presente*. *Gracias* to my friend María Luisa, for believing in me and cheering me on. *Gracias* to Leticia Trujillo, and Alicia Vélez, whose love, support, and shenanigans kept me grounded and gave me joy. *Gracias* to *mi pastor* Eugenio Torre, who has listened attentively, shepherded me in friendship, and grounded me in my vocation. *Gracias* to my church in Fajardo for your support and spiritual guidance. *Gracias* my pastor Laura Ruth for reading this work more times than anyone else, Benjamin Perkins, and the community of Hope Central Church in Jamaica Plain for supporting me in prayer. *Gracias* Theodore Hickman-Maynard for your accompaniment while writing and cheering me on. *Gracias* to Holly Benzenhafer for her edits, random encouragement texts in the middle of the night, and pastoring in friendship. *Gracias* for the company, support and friendship of Carmen Rodríguez, Karián Swayne, Stephanie Torres, Verónica Sosa, Monica Tzeng, Myron Kyrs, Abigail Díaz, Frankie García, Kate Common, Dorlimar Lebrón, Jonathan Resmini, Dan Hauge.

I am blessed and grateful to the Holy Spirit for weaving these words and these people in my journey. To all of those who accompanied me, *infinitas gracias*.

Hope is knowing that reality is not the exhaustion of all possibilities.

The Spirit weaves together the intentions of the people who lend themselves to be met by her.

List of Figures

5.1 Hope Axis Model Inward
5.2 Hope Axis Model Organization
5.3 Hope Axis Model Outward

Chapter One

About Context: "No Hay Mal que Dure Cien Años, Ni Cuerpo que lo Resista."

The Puerto Rican saying, "there is no evil that lasts a hundred years, nor a body that endures it," implies that either because of the passing of time or death, evil has an end; no misfortune, no evil lasts forever. Several articles and news stories about the island of Puerto Rico have identified a common sentiment of hopelessness among the Puerto Rican population living there and have located the source of that hopelessness in the ongoing socioeconomic and political crises created by government debt, colonialism, coloniality of power, and a significant population exodus to the United States in recent decades.[1] The destruction wrought by Hurricane María in September 2017 exacerbated an alreadydire situation. At the root of the evils haunting Puerto Rico—both its inhabitants and its diaspora—are the sins of colonialism, primarily its systems of economic exploitation, social stagnation, political oppression, and theft of land.[2] Fueling those colonialist sins are the practices of capitalism.[3] These practices are not only unsustainable, but they are also downright destructive. The material reality of the people, and the land affected by them, cannot endure such destruction. In this book, I develop a model of practice that can lead to the eradication of those evils, which for centuries has pervaded Puerto Rico and Puerto Ricans' livelihood and right to a dignified life. Rather than enduring another hundred years, I call for the abolition of colonial sins through liberation and practices of hope rather than through the deaths of bodies—persons—who can no longer withstand its effects.

This book is the result of ethnographic and practical theological research analyzed through several interdisciplinary lenses. This first chapter introduces both the project's method and the context of Puerto Rico to lay the foundations of both the theoretical approaches to hope and practice. I trace and analyze practices that embody and enact hope, many of which are informed and exemplified by the grassroots actions and ministries of local Christian churches working on the boundaries of official ecclesial institutions and denominations. I want to answer the question: How, in dialogue with and in response to the public sphere, does the Christian church currently participate in articulating and practicing a hopeful future, and how might it better do so? I begin by turning to history, specifically to the island's colonial roots.

PUERTO RICO'S COLONIAL ROOTS

Originally called Borikén by its indigenous inhabitants the *Taínos*, Puerto Rico made its appearance in European written history by way of the Spanish Empire's colonization in 1493. Never again would the locals be able to name themselves or decide their land's future.[4]

On May 25, 1898, during the Spanish-American War, US's future president Theodore Roosevelt wrote a letter to Senator Henry Cabot Lodge urging him not to agree to any peace treaty unless the United States gained (or annexed) Puerto Rico in the transaction.[5] The United States' paternalistic discourse around its acquisition of territories was painted as an altruistic act toward these assumed uncivilized countries.[6] However, Puerto Rico had been making headway with the socioeconomic advances of the time in its metropolis —depending on how one qualifies "progress." By the time the United States seized the opportunity to claim Puerto Rico as a colony, the island had abolished slavery (1873) and was in the process of becoming a sovereign country finally free from Spanish rule. The island's primary source of economic development was agriculture (tobacco, coffee, and sugar).[7] Although thinkers like Eugenio María De Hostos and Ramón Emeterio Betances, as well as some of the *criollo* elite, publicly denounced the "annexation" as a mistake, the promise of economic blossoming and the embrace of the United States was far too tempting for major local entrepreneurs.[8]

A variety of factors helped this process of acquisition. Though the United States wanted the island for military purposes, as it wished to control certain strategically situated naval stations, no one predicted the rise of the United States as a global power and its fabrication of a colonial empire, since this contradicted the principles of the USA's own founding revolution.[9] The entrepreneurial elite in Puerto Rico saw the United States as the epitome of democratic and progressive ideals. Before 1898, exiled Puerto Ricans living in New York had begun assimilating these progressive ideals, had stopped considering themselves Spaniards, and saw annexation as a political rupture with the past. Field workers and organizers saw an opportunity that would both accelerate their workers' movement and brake from the Spanish oppressive agricultural regime. Field owners, meanwhile, saw an opportunity to gain access to the sugar market in the United States of America along with financial protection from customs duties. The economic configuration that existed in the island would be radically altered with the arrival of the United States' regime.[10] Yet many Puerto Ricans saw the arrival of the United States through the promise of equal opportunities.

The role of "United States-as-colonizer" was not well received by many US leaders.[11] It seemed to them incompatible with the country's democratic foundation.[12] Racism was also rampant and the United States feared that a union with these occupied territories would lead to populating the nation with "inferior races."[13] Nonetheless, thoughts of economic and military exploitation drove intervention within and invasion of the island. In the Foraker Act (1900), Congress affirmed the US's domination over Puerto Rico and classified the island as a foreign territory. In this way it certified the constitutionality of colonialism as long as it was "liberal," in other words, as long as certain individual basic rights were respected.[14] In 1900, Puerto Ricans had not welcomed the idea of citizenship without the promise of statehood. The Jones Act was presented as bringing Puerto Rico a step closer. Through the Jones Act (1917), Puerto Ricans were granted citizenship within the United States of America.

The extension of US citizenship did not constitute a promise of statehood, but rather was an attempt to deterrent any consideration of political independence. The United States had just entered World War I, an event that only fed its desire to control Puerto Rico. The granting of citizenship justified Puerto Ricans' enlistment in the US military and the recruitment of Puerto Ricans for labor in the United States (because they would not have immigration restrictions and were considered cheap labor).[15] Strong proponents of statehood, such as politician Luis Muñoz Rivera, promoted a discourse of colonial dominance in the hopes of annexation, arguing that independence was an abstract ideal and that Puerto Rico was not capable of strong self-governance.[16] These first decades cemented the basis for Puerto Rico's future under colonial oppression, leading to systemic strategies that would make the US empire profit from the island's land and labor through plantation capitalism.[17]

THE PATH TO COLONIAL UNSUSTAINABILITY

Commonwealth of Puerto Rico and Operation Bootstrap

The establishment of the *Estado Libre Asociado* (Free Associated State or Commonwealth) in the 1950s, adopted with the "consent" of Puerto Ricans under this new territorial status, represented an attempt to comply with the United Nations after World War II to eliminate Puerto Rico's official colonial status. This arrangement weakened the independence movement and it temporarily suppressed the conversation about Puerto Rico becoming a state.[18] Regardless, from 1948 to 1957, a gag law silenced—though it did not eradicate—dissidence against the US government; it was a felony to display the Puerto Rican flag. The emerging effect of "Commonwealth" status on Puerto Rico would become a driving source of its struggles and consternations. Puerto Rico was not established as a US state, and therefore was not meant to be free nor associate, but rather a "common good" for the United States, as the term "commonwealth" in English itself indicates.

For years, the U.S. government had been using Puerto Rico as a source for its economic development, a practice that solidified with the implementation of "Operation Bootstrap" in the 1950s, which laid the groundwork for the island's current socioeconomic debacle. Operation Bootstrap aimed to transition the island from an agricultural to an industrial economy without considering the economy already in place. The United States saw the economic value in the island's geographical location and exploited it, making Puerto Rico the first "third world country" to develop as an export-led industry. The Puerto Rican government signed off on the implementation of this project due to its promise of economic flourishing. For a period of time, the project did offer economic growth; however, this was not sustainable. Due to Puerto Rico's territorial status, local and federal environmental laws have always been less strict than those within the United States, leading to significant environmental degradation and destruction. As Déborah Berman Santana writes, "proponents of Operation Bootstrap-type development have argued that environmental damage is a necessary evil when we face the urgent economic and social need to provide jobs."[19]

These reforms were not happening in isolation from the rest of the United States' politics with other Latin American countries. As Berman Santana notes, "when the Cuban revolution of 1959 presented a socialist and nationalist model for Latin America, Puerto Rico served as Washington's anti-Cuba model."[20] In light of Puerto Rico's newfound purpose during the 1950s—to enable the United States to expand and dominate the market of the Americas—Puerto Rico also became the "poster child" for "non-nationalistic economic development."[21] Cuba and Puerto Rico shared a strong cultural and political bond, as well as their common struggle for independence from Spain (*Grito de Yara* and *Grito de Lares* respectively). With the demonization of communism and the threat of withdrawal of United States' support, the narrative among Puerto Ricans after *La Revolución* in Cuba was ignited by the fear that Puerto Ricans would suffer a similar fate. The United States, meanwhile, intended Puerto Rico to become an economic and political model for the rest of the "third world," but it did not take into account that its core strategies would not work in politically independent countries.[22] U.S. industries, incentivized with the promise of cheap island labor and tax breaks, began to relocate to the island, bringing materials from the United States along with them.[23] These practies of importing material and providing tax exemptions to foreign companies continue in Puerto Rico to this day with the vulturine of disaster capitalism. They are two of the primary reasons for Puerto Rico's currently broken finances, which are not based on the growth of a sustainable local economy. But broken local systems were always part of the U.S. plan for Puerto Rico, as is shown by Operation Bootstrap's goals for the island after World War II:

> First, the pre-empting of any possibility for independence, which could possibly threaten U.S. plans for the island; second, the gutting of economic development programs already operating on the island which emphasized land expropriation and redistribution, government-run agricultural and industrial enterprises, and the public takeover of utilities—all of which were denounced as "dangerously socialistic" by Congress, and which were thought to discourage private American investment (Goodsell, 1967:39–40); third, the shift by Fomento from aiding new local enterprises to offering incentives to relocating U.S. firms, and a more complete integration of the insular economy into that of the mainland; fourth, the local suppression of independent labor unions which would undermine the "docility" of the workforce, an important incentive for foreign investment (Pantojas Garcia, 1979: 102); and fifth, support for a development program which would create some jobs and raise the average standard of living, thus undercutting support for independence and reinforcing the propaganda that the island could not survive as an independent state.[24]

Because of its economic implications, this program created a division between people who were against the United States' settlement and those who were not, but it also created a sense of loyalty to the "good work" the United States was doing in Puerto Rico. I remember my grandmother used to say that the first Puerto Rican elected governor, Luis Muñoz Marín, *"le puso sus primeros zapatos."*[25] Operation Bootstrap happened with the aid of Luis Muñoz Marín and the *Partido Popular Democrático* (PPD).[26] This political party, created in 1939, sought "land reform and rural resettlement, government-sponsored import substitution industrialization and largely autonomous economic development leading to eventual political independence."[27] Operation Bootstrap represented the financial support this movement needed to achieve their populist goals.

However, once in power, their goal of future economic and political independence for Puerto Rico went out the window. The PPD focused on guaranteeing financial support from the United States.[28] As a result, today Puerto Rico has a culture of economic and political dependence. 75 to 90 percent of the food consumed by locals is imported; the welfare system disables people from achieving upward mobility, rendering them yet more stigmatized to the United States and to local elites; the practice of privatizing public properties and services increases living expenses; and the restrictions on importation/exportation and the instability of the market with foreign companies make it difficult to hope.[29] After the 2008 financial crisis in the United States, companies already established on the island (pharmaceuticals, for example) left with haste accelerated their flight, creating rampant unemployment. A year after that, former governor Luis Fortuño, put in place Law 7, which allowed the declaration of a state of emergency and with it laying off 30,000 government employees. Before that, however, with the end of the tax window of Law 936 in 2006, it was possible to see the island's economic deterioration making headlines. Law 936 contributed to the economic crisis in PR during and after its tenure. It was effective from 1976 to 1996 and provided federal tax exemptions to foreign investors. Once the provision of the law ended officially in 2006, foreign companies left the island. For many Puerto Ricans, the moral discouragement of realizing they have little or no agency in their development is pervasive and unrelenting.

Puerto Rican Catholic theologian Teresa Delgado traces this feeling of moral discouragement in her book *A Puerto Rican Decolonial Theology: Prophesy Freedom*. Delgado's work engages the literature of Puerto Rican authors in the diaspora. In her analysis of Esmeralda Santiago's novel *Almost a Woman*, she makes the heart-wrenching comparison of the female protagonist—a battered woman belittled by and codependent on her abusive lover—to Puerto Rico.[30] In this analogy, Puerto Rico has given up its will to be free. Its dependence on the United States has thwarted it from believing or imagining a future in which it can live on its own. In what ways does this comparison hold true? In Puerto Rico, agriculture and local entrepreneurship were abandoned as major economic drivers, and both land and people in effect began to be sold to the highest bidder. Military structures and facilities on the island, and Puerto Ricans' enlistment in the military, contained the unemployment crisis and injected substantial funds into the island's economy.[31] After many years of struggling and petitioning the United States government to retire its Military Training Camp from the town of Vieques because of the high incidence of cancer and the environmental impact left behind, the *viequenses* are now dealing with the withdrawal of the economic boost, along with the lasting consequences of ecological and human harm wrought by remaining environmental contamination.

The shifts in Puerto Rico's local economy and its exportation of human capital have been predicated on the revenue interests of the United States, not its own. The transition from an agricultural economy to an industrial economy in the 1950s and the attempts to assimilate the island to this shift, which led to its government's bankruptcy, are both major signs of these external interests. According to a 2019 analysis of 101 countries by *The World Bank*, Puerto Rico has the third-greatest economic inequality.[32] The machinations of colonial enterprise do not only pervade the economic and material present and future of Puerto Ricans and island locals, but also impoverish the embodiment and promise of liberation, the flourishing of the *Imago Dei*, and theological imagination in its midst.[33] The United Statesian colonial and assimilation enterprises used religious institutions to further their economic and political agendas, deeply impacting and transforming the island's religious makeup.

Religious History (1898–1930) and Political Implications

Although there were religious dissidents, Puerto Rico's majority was culturally and religiously Roman Catholic at the beginning of the twentieth century. Catholicism was the official religion of the island. The United States saw the Church as an enemy because of its alliance with Catholic Spain and labeled its institutions and practices as problems of national security. Within months after the U.S.A. settled on the island, half the Spanish Catholic clergy had fled, and the separation of church and state was enforced. Immediately, Protestant missionaries migrated to the island of Puerto Rico —as it happened thrughout Latin America— to preach the gospel and assist in the process of cultural assimilation; evangelization and cultural imperialism were inseparable. Protestant churches and missionaries saw the Spanish-American war as an opportunity to fulfill the "great commission" of universal evangelization and, according to Silva Gotay's research, to speed up the Second Coming of Christ.

Even the Catholic Church consented to the United States' intervention once the Vatican's petition for the protection of Catholic territories failed.[34] When the Paris Treaty was signed, the Vatican had assigned a papal delegate to ensure the Catholic Church's interests on the island were maintained.[35] Cultural chauvinism also mattered. United Statesian priest, Dennis O'Connell, wrote an article in the journal *Catholic World* in support of the United States' invasion, arguing that God uses different nations in different moments and that, in this case, Spanish principles were unable to guide Puerto Rican civilization to the future.[36] Monsignor Louis Chapelle was given the task of helping assimilate the Caribbean dioceses to the U.S.A.'s culture. Chapelle, in turn, assigned Bishop Joseph Blenk, who implemented curricula that fomented this process among students, expecting that curricula would eventually mix with the Church's politics. Both the Catholic and (to a greater extent) the Protestant Churches, therefore, contributed to the United States' nationalist expansionism *"al sacralizar los procesos politicos de imposición cultural, militar y política sobre Puerto Rico."*[37]

The United State's military regime intervened in all of the island's public services, but especially in the public-school system. They believed this was the best way to reorient the population's loyalty toward the United States and its occupation. The military government also encouraged the expansion of Protestant missions, believing that it was critical for the assimilation of Puerto Ricans that their cultural values be reframed through a Protestant lens. As this process gained traction through both public and religious education, the U.S.A.'s government also debilitated local property owners to decrease their political power.[38]

Pro-assimilation Catholics on the island nonetheless battled against Protestantism. Unable to distinguish between faith and culture, the United States' project of using (Protestant) missionary religion to promote assimilation received much pushback from the Catholic Church.[39] Catholics began to articulate and express Catholicism at the core of Puerto Rican culture.[40] When it discovered that the U.S. ideals of progress, fulfillment, happiness, and justice were not to be applied in the island, the Catholic Church widened the gap between assimilation and the affirmation of a distinctly Puerto Rican identity.

However, Puerto Rican nationalist sentiment was already present before the United States took control. This is evident, for example, in upstart movements like 1868's *El Grito de Lares*. At this time, the Catholic Church had begun substituting *criollo* elites for Spanish priests in order to contain nationalist sentiment; still, the seed had been planted. A longing for political independence thus began spreading through the island, including among the Catholic laity, well before the U.S.A.'s colonization. In 1912, the *Partido de la Independencia* was founded, followed by decades of intellectual ferment in service of the affirmation of a Puerto Rican identity. Already by the 1920s, *ponceño* Pedro Albizu Campos, a Harvard Law School graduate and veteran turned primary promoter of Puerto Rico's independence, understood the Catholic faith as consubstantial with Puerto Rican identity.[41]

In 1925, the island had approximately 160 priests—of whom only twelve were Puerto Rican. Albizu Campos understood this as a weakness in advancing a nationalist agenda. The Protestant churches, meanwhile, were primarily pastored by natives, due to the outmigration of U.S.A.–born Protestant pastors after a series of hurricanes.[42] While the Catholic church was shaping Puerto Rico's political and cultural resistance, the Protestant church infiltrated *lo cotidiano* (the day-to-day) by enabling access and direct exposure to the Bible. Not only that, Protestant missionaries proactively promoted literacy, especially in the rural areas. In this and other ways, U.S. Protestantism helped sacralize the imperial movement of economic expansion in the late nineteenth and twentieth centuries.[43]

If it is possible to identify extremes—the Catholic Church aligned with cultural and political nationalism and Protestant churches with assimilation and statehood—in the early decades of the U.S.A.'s control of Puerto Rico, these postures are less obvious in twenty-first-century society. Nonetheless, the political and the religious remain deeply intertwined. For renowned Puerto Rican sociologist of religion Samuel Silva Gotay, as long as religious practices, concepts, and attitudes enable the organization of life in society, the church will have political implications.[44] I continue to explore this notion throughout this book, since the political and economic context created by colonization and coloniality of power is responsible for the hopelessness that has become embedded in Puerto Rican society and identity.

P.R.O.M.E.S.A.

The dire situation of the economic and sociopolitical climate of Puerto Rico escalated, or, rather, discovered a level below rock bottom in 2016. P.R.O.M.E.S.A. (the acronym, meaning "promise" in Spanish, for "Puerto Rico Oversight, Management, and Economic Stability Act") is a 2016 United States federal law authorizing oversight and restructuring of the island's financial practices in order to repay the over $72 billion debt the government had acquired due to vulture funds. A vulture fund is a hedge fund where a third-party invests in weak debt, acquired at a discounted rate to make a profit from the organization who owned on the original debt. There is a saying: *"Del árbol caído, todos hacen leña"* (From the fallen tree, we all make firewood.). Puerto Rico's debt is "triple tax-exempt." That means owners of the bonds don't face federal, state or local taxes on the interest they earn."[45] Over the last decade, therefore, investors continued to buy the island's debt, even though this practice only deepened the financial crisis and forced Puerto Rico to pay higher loan rates, which in turn attracted yet more investors. P.R.O.M.E.S.A. established an oversight committee (the Financial Oversight and Management Board of Puerto Rico, or *La Junta de Control Fiscal*) that has the power to approve and veto the island's budget—in other words, more power than its governor. It was only in 1949 that Puerto Ricans had started to elect their governors; P.R.O.M.E.S.A. reminded them that their "short lived agency" was merely an illusion. The law established austerity measures, projected to last until 2026, that reduced pensions, health care, and education expenditures in order to repay creditors.

Lawyer Fermín Arraiza warned his readers what would likely happen as a result of implementing P.R.O.M.E.S.A.:

> Mientras la población emigra y se nos muere, aquí seguirán llegando multimillonarios haciendo negocios, comprando y restaurando edificios, sobre todo en zonas históricas y turísticas, gracias a los incentivos de la Ley 20 y 21. El plan no es meramente pagar a los bonistas. La agenda es suplantar la población con multimillonarios extranjeros y reducirnos a minoría. Nadie tendrá el capital para regresar. Puerto Rico dejará de ser una opción económica para los puertorriqueños. Los que nos quedemos seremos los nuevos sirvientes. Deleitaremos a la nueva clase social con nuestros bailes típicos de bomba, danza y plena. Y sí, se le pagará a los bonistas mientras nos aniquilan como pueblo.[46]

Concern over this fate led to legal challenges, but on July 13, 2018, federal judge Laura Taylor Swain ruled that Puerto Rico's status as a territory allows laws and regulations to override the U.S.A.'s Constitution. Puerto Rico is not fully protected by the Constitution, allowing federal entities to proceed differently in its territories.[47]

This is not the first time that Puerto Rico has experienced this form of systemic supervision. In 1899, after hurricane San Ciriaco, General Davis developed an agency (*Junta de Caridad*) to distribute provisions to the poor people who had been gravely affected by this phenomenon. At the same time, he rejected Coll y Toste's proposal for providing agricultural loans to local businesspeople. He also rejected the facilitation of short-and long-term loans, knowing that this would accelerate the process of bankruptcy and allow assets and lands to be sold to United States investors.[48] When the United States invaded in 1898, 93 percent of Puerto Ricans owned their own land. Because of the freezing of credit lines and denegation of loans, most lost these lands in short order. The U.S.A. enforced dedication of the lands to monoculture, and the elimination of sustainable agricultural practices contributed to the destruction of small farms and local producers, increasing the need for imported goods.[49] Under the military regime, the exportation of goods (tobacco, sugar, and coffee) increased exponentially compared to the period under Spanish rule. Despite this increase in goods sold, labor exploitation was clearly visible in salaries, which perpetuated and indeed increased poverty among Puerto Ricans.[50] More than a century later, the insufficient organization of FEMA, undistributed resources, and the refusal to eliminate the Jones Act of 1920 suffocated the rehabilitation of the island and the islanders after Hurricane María.[51] The present state of affairs in Puerto Rico is no coincidence. Only a few days after María struck, one of the first tweets from the United States president was a reminder of Puerto Rico's debt and its stalled repayment.[52]

Hurricane María

On the night of September 19, 2017, I was on the phone with my mother in Puerto Rico, going through our hurricane-preparedness checklist. She said she loved me, and that she was going to *hacer el rosario* (pray the rosary) and go to bed. From my place in Boston, I figured that the only way I could be with her was by praying the rosary at the same time. The mysteries for that day were *los misterios dolorosos*—the sorrowful mysteries. Sometimes I did not know to which María I was praying. María passed through an island that was already only just holding on to its loincloth, and left it naked.[53] As the cyclone roared with the force of a tornado, threatening to blow open doors and windows, and in many homes devastatingly succeeding, my sister replayed in her mind an emergency exit strategy. If she put the smaller dog on her back, she could with one arm grab the larger dog and with the other hold on to my mother as they ran out to safety. Assuming there would be any safety to be found, but she couldn't plan that far ahead. Sadly, the hurricane was only the beginning.

The *New York Times* profiled the emotional and mental state of Puerto Ricans on the island in an interview with clinical psychologist Dr. Carlos del Toro Ortíz. María marked the conjuncture and inevitable unravelling of all of Puerto Rico's centennial sorrows. In his close to twenty years of clinical practice, Dr. del Toro said, he "had never before hospitalized as many people with suicidal and homicidal thoughts in such a short period of time."[54] People experienced long hours of terror as María made its way through the island, destroying their crops, infrastructure, fauna and flora, homes, and lives. In the aftermath, Del Toro shared, "When it starts raining, [people on the island] have episodes of anxiety because they think their house is going to flood again. They have heart palpitations, sweating, catastrophic thoughts. They think 'I'm going to drown,' 'I'm going to die,' 'I'm going to lose everything.'"[55] For Del Toro, returning to a routine is key to overcoming trauma. And although I agree with his professional assessment, questions linger. The routine of "what used to be" was hard enough; what on earth could moving forward look like?

The government investigated the post-María rise in suicides and the relationship between the event and trauma.[56] Officially, thirty-seven suicide cases were reported post-María. The Administration of Mental Health and Addiction Services (ASSMCA) reported that in September 2017 they received 4,473 calls, of which 611 were related to suicidal ideation or conduct. In October, they received fewer calls (3,975), but nonetheless 792 cases of people with suicidal tendencies or thoughts. In comparison with the previous year's suicide statistics, there had been a 17.19 percent increase in suicides.

Extreme trauma marked many islanders' experience. There were people whose family members died in the midst of the hurricane who had to live with the decomposing bodies for days because there was no one who could pick up the corpse. The government authorized 911 cremations with no autopsy in October 2017,[57] but the number of deaths caused by the hurricane and its aftermath is much higher than officially reported.[58] On the island, one finds people who have lost everything, people whose families are being disintegrated in the aftermath. The situation has also disrupted the routine of people with mental illness and developmental conditions, exacerbating the emotional and mental precariousness of the population. This catastrophe will shape and change the course of the island's history.

In María's aftermath, people from around the world, and especially the Puerto Rican diaspora, extended themselves and their resources to aid the island and the islanders. They became the hope of the people on the island. Ellen Ott Marshall argues that people cannot have hope in God if they do not have hope in humanity.[59] I wrestle with this, knowing that humankind is not always so kind. However, I agree that who we are, what we do, and how we let the God of life work through us enacts the hope of the hopeless. Hoping in humanity demonstrates how humanity is connected and dependent on each other, dependent on community. In the wake of the trauma of María, islanders and "diasporicans" have carried their pain and affliction, and pushing through for their own sakes and for the sake of their siblings.[60]

Verano del '19

As material, emotional, and spiritual recovery continued in Puerto Rico, writers, journalists, and scholars have begun compiling the stories of islanders and diasporicans and their experiences before, during, and after the hurricane. The impact of the colonial enterprise and its pairing with an inept local government reached to the tipping point of the uproar of *el pueblo puertorriqueño* in the summer of 2019 when a Telegram chat between the then-governor, Ricardo Roselló, elected officials and government agency directors made the news. In this chat officials mocked *el pueblo* and those who died in the hurricane among other egregious conversations. *Aquí fue donde la puerca entorchó el rabo.*[61] For fifteen days, hundreds of thousands of people marched towards the capitol demanding the resignation of the governor. These manifestations were covered around the world and Puerto Ricans residing outside of the island flew in to march in protest. Even religious sectors publicly denounced the government; some of those of unprecedented character.

Rafael Bernabé and Manuel Rodríguez state in their analysis that the summer of 2019 gave *"al país un sentido de posibilidad: el sentimiento de que las cosas pueden cambiar, de que las cosas se pueden cambiar, de que la gente, movilizándose en la calle, las puede cambiar.*"[62] The authors point out that the massive and unprecedented mobilization of the Puerto Rican people and allies was demonstrated in hundreds to thousands (from July 10 to 14 in Fortaleza), to 20 or 30 thousand (on July 15 in the Capitol and in Fortaleza), to about 400 thousand (on July 17 from the Capitol to the Totem), to about one million (on July 22 in Hato Rey). It was 15 days of incessant and intense protests under the slogan "*Ricky Renuncia*" (Ricky, quit) in a collective, diverse, creative, sound or sign language, in the ringing of drums, *pleneros* or pots and pans, rhythmic and danceable, poetic, secular, religious, dispersed throughout the country and outside of it, taking over the air, maritime and land space.[63] Finally, on July 24, 2019, Governor Ricardo (Ricky) Rosselló Nevares announced his resignation, effective as of August 2, 2019.[64]

HOPE, THEOLOGY, AND THE CHURCH

My work addresses multiple layers of socioeconomic and political circumstances that produce hopelessness by examining the sources of hope on which local Puerto Rican churches rely; ecclesial discourses on hope; and churches' practices of hope. Hurricane María exposed the island, revealing a situation that for decades has been eroding Puerto Ricans' hope and spirit. Though I do not aim to find a starting point of decline, the market crash of 2008, the billion-dollar debt, ongoing poverty, persistent lack of employment opportunities, insufficient health services, and a host of oppressive U.S. policies related to Puerto Rico's colonial status, have negatively impacted both island and islanders' vision for the future. They have hindered hope. Not to mention the most recent struggles of these past couple of years with Covid-19 and the healthcare inequities, as well as exotification of island tourism by United Statesians during this time of travel restrictions.

In this historical moment in Puerto Rico, where and what are the practices of hope? What does hope look like? At present, one pervasive practice of "hope" for many people on the island is mass departure.[65] Hope is manifested by leaving since, for many, there is none-to-little hope to be found on the island. This is not a commentary on migration, which is a human right and experience, rather an observation that migration as forced displacement causes an even more profound sense of hopelessness about the future of Puerto Rico as a country, along with a lack of imagination and a sense of impotence. In the decade following the financial crisis, hundreds of thousands left the island; in the month after María struck, over fifty-eight thousand people fled and Puerto Ricans continue to fly out as wealthy United Statesians and disaster capitalists looking for tax breaks fly in.[66] There is pain, shame, and suffering in the face of the dismemberment from dreams, land, and family for those who leave and those who remain; the new *Lamento Borincano* happens at the airport.[67]

By understanding the real means (practices) of producing hope, and how those practices are sustained, I hope to offer the church, as an organized body in Puerto Rico but also beyond, a better sense of how one can live into hope. Theologies of hope often establish a connection between hope and liberation—seeing liberation as the outcome of hope. I will explore what that looks like in a Puerto Rican context. Further, I bring a communitarian lens to my analysis of hope, meaning that I will not only be focusing on what individuals (for example, pastors) say, do, or believe; rather, I will interact with communities and look at communal worship, rituals, wisdom, and practices. I contend that hope must be understood *in* community, just as liberation is always enacted in community. Liberation from what? one might ask. Liberation from the evils that oppress and ravish our body(ies) is the answer.

In addition to identifying hope, I ask why the church and its discourse of hope may not be connecting with people and, therefore, not inspiring practices of hope. Are there gaps between what the church is saying or offering, on one hand, and what the people are experiencing, on the other? Christian ethicist Ellen Ott Marshall speaks about a "responsible" theology of hope.[68] I build on her concept of responsible hope and move it forward by also arguing for *sustainable* practices of hope—practices that go beyond wishful thinking or inflated optimisms, and yet are still hopeful.

I am also curious about the extent to which Christian hope can be practiced in public, responsibly and justly. What is the public good news offered by the church in Puerto Rico? For Gustavo Gutiérrez, the church is a journeying people of God; this journey happens in history, and it happens in public.[69] Can the church's enactment of hope connect to, learn from, and respond to cries for hope outside the church? I believe that hope is an integral aspect of the church's presence in and with the world. The colonial tyranny of the United States' government is killing Puerto Rican hope for the sake of empire, with aid of the local government. When the church partakes publicly in a people's struggle, the hope of the church meets the hope of a society in desperate need of flourishing.

In *Embracing Hopelessness*, Miguel De La Torre argues that hope hinders liberation and is a source of oppression.[70] He says that hope is not the apparent ethos of the disenfranchised but rather is "imposed by those who might be endangered if the marginalized were instead to act. . . . The first step toward liberation requires the crucifixion of hope—for as long as hope exists, the world's wretched have something to lose, and thus will not risk all to change the social structures."[71] I argue, however, that the enactment of hope in the context of Puerto Rico is both the means and the source of liberation. By this I mean that living out a sustainable hope will feed society's future hope and thus enact liberation, even beyond this context. The practical theological solution is not to abandon the concept of hope, but to re-think the context in which hope operates as a vehicle for liberation. The research undergirding this book articulates an understanding of hope in this context that transcends traditional eschatologies in which Christian hope is a distraction from liberation or a source of oppression. The hope against which De La Torre argues is indeed oppressive. But Hurricane María has awakened a sense of hope and resilience in Puerto Rican people both inside and outside the island.[72] At the same time, María undermined hope. Accepting this paradox, I argue that the hope that has been both challenged and unveiled is a false hope, an illusion, giving Puerto Rico the opportunity to articulate and delve deeper into truer and more sustainable hopes for its future.

The motto in the post-María reality—though not free of critique— became #Puerto Rico se levanta (Puerto Rico rises).[73] Rubem Alves argues that for true liberation to happen, the Organization must die; "we need to be born again."[74] By this, Alves means that society needs to destroy its "Organizations" and begin again. In many ways, the Puerto Rican context is an ideal microcosm for understanding what it would mean to find hope within a society that is being born again. Yet this is no naïve understanding of being born again. It does not mean that society is being created from scratch, nor that birthing and midwifing this restructuring will not be filled with perils and trials. The socioeconomic, political, and colonial debacle intertwined with the neoliberal and capitalist culture on the island drags down the process of recuperation and rebirth. The opportunity of "starting over" is nonetheless helpful for glimpsing what it would mean to die and resurrect (Jn. 3:3) as a society. What would it mean to start from a place of hope and liberation?

There is hope in this death because "the present evil needs to die for a new creation to arise."[75] Puerto Rico's infrastructure systems—its electric system, water system, health system, road system, communication system, and so forth—were destroyed or are on the verge of collapsing. Given this destruction, different and new alternatives await. There are hopes of being able to make things better. And, after all, the infrastructure Puerto Rico had in place was not so great to begin with. Yet the process of hope and rebirth does not begin with a blank slate. The soft and hard powers of neocolonialism, colonialism, economic extortion, and opportunism are still in play and need to be viewed with suspicion, as witnessed by the revelation that the energy company that was granted a $300 million contract in 2017 to rebuild the electrical grid of Puerto Rico had connections to the Trump administration.[76] However, Puerto Rico is also on the verge of great opportunities, identifying the revolutionary practices of hope grounded in the work of deep systemic change. Further, it is the poor who can determine what these practices are, for, as Alves would say, it is the poor and disenfranchised who can envision and enact the practices of hope; it is those who are living under the conditions created by a broken neoliberal and capitalist system who truly have something to lose, contrary to what De La Torre argues. One cannot lose the material stability and flourishing that has never been afforded to them.

In this current climate of uncertainty in the aftermath of Hurricane María, Puerto Rican people—indeed all persons of good will—are challenged to understand deeply what their hope is and where it is found, including the elasticity of its endurance or, contrarily, the surrendering to hopelessness. The struggle to hope and envision a new future allows us to explore the possibilities of imagination and develop a deeper understanding of a sustainable hope and, at the same time, define an eschatological hope.

STRUCTURE

The layout of this book is a weaving of spirals of concepts that imagine hope at the center of being, and is shaped by the interactions of approaches and fields here present. Though each chapter builds on the previous one, I invite you to understand the methodology as a nonlinear journey. The overarching research method of this book is a form of practical theology. The search I have articulated above for hope and its understanding invites—indeed requires—a liberating hermeneutic.[77] As a researcher, this places me in a position in which, for the sake of the integrity of the findings, I need not only outline my method but also disclose how my commitments, lenses, and starting point interact with the research. I hypothesize that my findings will both unveil and contribute to a theology of hope in the context of Puerto Rico. I am approaching this research with particular theoretical lenses and an understanding of hope through particular markers. These markers differentiate certain kinds of hope as distractions and others as liberative. I argue for them in the last part of this book, which proposes the articulation of a model for practices of hope in the service of a *proyecto de país* (national project). The work is divided in three parts: theoretical framework, qualitative research, and model construction.

Part one: Theoretical Framework. In the first part I develop a theoretical framework that proceeds from a historical analysis of the church in Puerto Rico. I rely on Puerto Rican literature and theology, in conversation with, among others, Teresa Delgado, Samuel Silva Gotay, Luis Rivera Pagán, and Doris Pizzarro. The work of my interlocutors describes and traces religious, colonial, and grassroots community activism in the island of Puerto Rico from 1898 to the present.

This historical framework establishes a basis for thinking about hope and its challenges. This analysis sets the stage for articulating contextual understandings of hope in dialogue with theologians of hope such as Rubem Alves, Ellen Ott Marshall, and Jürgen Moltmann. The collaborators I interview in my qualitative study (described further below) resort to types of discourse and refer to popular religious practices and artistic productions that they understand as expressing or enacting hope.[78] This discourse and these practices cannot be understood apart from the various forms of public and religious imaginary operative in the island. Therefore, I engage examples from popular culture that help us understand that imaginary. Though Christianity is not the only religion practiced in Puerto Rico, I specifically want to understand how the church participates in public space, engaging in hopeful practices or practices that bring about hope (for the church and the wider society). Although some individuals in Puerto Rico attempt to divide sacred from secular space, one cannot divorce our epistemological frameworks from what is embedded in us as people who share a culture. In both spaces, people are marked by shared culture and memory; understanding the underpinnings of how this operates is vital for uncovering hope's sources. Therefore, literature that explores the intersections of hope, imagination, and memory supports this work.

Postcolonial and decolonial theologies are essential to understanding how Puerto Rico's colonial history plays a role in contemporary society and church practices. Ever since its reconception as la *Isla de San Juan Bautista* in the late fifteenth century, Puerto Rico has developed a culture and an identity of political and economic dependency, as well as a colonized mindset. Postcolonial theory and theology unveil the dynamics of colonialism and might give us a push further into a hopeful future. Political and public theologies, meanwhile, allow me to read space and place, as well as understand the political dimensions and impact of the church's public acts. Liberation theologies provide epistemological and hermeneutical frameworks for the development of my distinctive practical theological approach. This first section is the most extensive not because it is the most important, but because it lays out my method as a writer and thinker. Although I have a clear understanding of how I expect hope to be liberative, I do not want to propose a unidirectional trajectory and definition of hope. Rather I want to weave fields, disciplines, and concepts with hope at the center, not at the end. Hope is an axis.

Part two: Qualitative Research. The second part of this book includes direct qualitative research and consists of data collected through one-on-one interviews, site visits, field notes, and document analysis. I visited Puerto Rico and was a participant-observer in the community outreach programs, practices, and sermons of six congregations in the northeast area of the island.

The data I gathered focused on the topic of hope and on congregational practices and discourses that enact and express hope.

I examined these Catholic, Mainline Protestant, Pentecostal, and independent churches: San Francis of Assisi Catholic Church in Old San Juan, Christian Church Disciples of Christ in Fajardo, Mar Azul independent church in Guaynabo, La Travesía Presbyterian church (PCA) in San Juan, Iglesia de Dios Pentecostal MI in Rio Piedras, and Primera Iglesia Bautista de Carolina. I looked at the discourse and practice of these congregations in order to shed light on how they attempt to inform a public imagination toward hope. In addition to my visits and interviews, I examined documents such as public statements, websites, and related blogs, as well as archived and recorded sermons when available. This document analysis enriched the descriptive aspect of my research and provided a deeper understanding of hope as expressed in these congregations' theological discourse.[79]

Part three: Model Construction. The final part of this book is constructive. Analyzing my qualitative research findings in light of and in dialogue with my theoretical framework, I develop a model of hope, a recipe, that has particular markers of what I suggest is a liberative and sustainable hope. The unearthing of these markers includes, but is not limited to, responses to the following questions: Does ecclesial practice, production, or discourse denote an expectation for the future? Does the discourse of hope understand and take into account the material reality of a particular situation? Does it model a pedagogy of solidarity?[80] Does it foster liberation, imagination, and flourishing? Can this hope be shared across social and religious divisions?[81]

As with this first chapter, the next four are prompted by and titled with Puerto Rican sayings and idiomatic expressions.[82] This is not just a personal or aesthetic choice but speaks to the importance and depth of folk knowledge, which permeates my work, and without which my content would be an empty shell. Chapter 2 includes a brief literature review of theologies of hope. I define categories of hope as ontological and virtuous. To provide context for my discussion of present-day practices of hope, I also perform a brief historical and comparative analysis of Hurricanes San Felipe (1928) and San Cipriano (1932), during which all agriculture and many lives were lost, creating economic despair and our first major wave of immigration from the island to the United States. Chapter 3 presents my findings on practices of hope in the present situation in Puerto Rico. This chapter argues for the centrality of hope in the work of the church for humanity and creation's flourishing, and shows how the churches I studied in Puerto Rico embody this work. My analysis is in conversation with the history of the Christian church in Puerto Rico and its participation in current social movements. Chapter 4 explores hope in relation to memory, postcolonial analysis and imagination, with *la lucha* as its precondition.[83] Here I follow Rubem Alves's claim that the imagination of a new and liberated future can only come from the oppressed.[84] In Puerto Rico, in the wake of Hurricane María, when folks are asked how they are, they respond *"en la lucha."* The only way to hope for a new future, I argue, is through the memory of what is possible and the imagination of what could be. Chapter 5 develops a model for hope, a new hermeneutic. It presents two models for hope as it articulates my conclusions from a practical theological perspective and accentuates the liberative epistemological and practical aspects of hope.

CONCLUSION

As Hurricane María became a marker in Puerto Rican history, Puerto Rico might be stuck on the "sorrowful mysteries" for a very long time, but that does not mean it does not continue to move forward, like the rosary, bead by bead. November 19, 2017, commemorated the island's "discovery" by Spain 524 years previous; and in the Catholic Church it is also the day of the patron virgin of Puerto Rico, the Virgin of the Divine Providence. This date also marked two months after the hurricane. Offering a glimpse of the historical and theological complexities of coloniality, my mother called me on that morning of November 19 to remind me of how María (the virgin) gave us Jesús, the embodiment of divine providence. Jesús is with us and in us, and when Jesús is in us, we show up. *Los buenos somos más,* she reminded me; people are showing up, and we are rising together.[85] This was the first time my mom had cried with me after María. Paradoxically, the realization of hope was what finally allowed her to break down in tears.[86] To claim, with the wisdom of Puerto Rican folk knowledge, that "there is no evil that lasts a hundred years, nor a body that endures it" is no naïve confession of the eradication of evil. Rather, the statement is catalytic, compelling us to imagine that evil is not all there is and that a flourishing future is possible. Here I aim to expose the different practices and ways in which one can begin to glimpse a sustainable theology of hope, and propose a model that can be put into practice.

Chapter Two

About Hope: "Al Mal Tiempo, Buena Cara"

"*Al mal tiempo, buena cara*": in times of adversity (literally: bad times or bad weather), put on a good face. Likewise, the essence of the gift of hope is perseverance.[1] When people are able to face hardship with *buena cara*, there must be something grounding them. There must be something they know or feel that holds them in place to act forward. I believe this "something" is hope. With this in mind, I address a theology and understanding of hope, exploring how it relates to the Puerto Rican context in the face of hope's demise.

I begin this chapter by outlining both the concepts that allegedly negate hope (hopelessness, desperation, and despair) and those that simulate hope (optimism and positivity) to help declutter, separate, and hone a definition of hope that can speak truth to the needs of the people in ways that are grounding and sustainable. Having decluttered hope by distinguishing it from its negations and simulations, I then turn to an interrogation of hope. This interrogation is threefold.

First, I ask: What is hope? I seek to define the concept by drawing upon theologies of hope from Jürgen Moltmann, Ellen Ott Marshall, and Rubem Alves. I also incorporate challenges to those theologies, noting that theological understandings of *what we hope for* are deeply connected to people's contingent contexts. This last point will be examined in the next chapter. In *this* chapter, what is most important is how hope functions, not what hope says.

My second question: Where is the hope? Here, I search for the source of hope. My exposition distinguishes hope as ontological and connected to one's power of imagination and practice. Finally, I ask: What does hope look like? In this section, I begin to articulate ecclesial practices that I will develop more fully in the qualitative section of Chapter 3. Here I argue that hope looks like the practices of Christian service and community engagement. Although hope is not limited to these practices, through them hope is possible in the face of adversity. To give body to this statement, I use the historical example of the 1930s revival following two devastating hurricanes in Puerto Rico.

DECLUTTERING HOPE

Hopelessness, Desperation, and Despair

Hope allows space for hopelessness. As an exercise in semiotics, I begin by articulating what negates hope in order to understand what it *is*. What prompts me to do so is a concern spiked after reading *Embracing Hopelessness* by ethicist Miguel De La Torre. De La Torre focuses on a "hope" fueled by white Christian hegemonic theology, pointing toward Eurocentric ways of understanding and seeing salvation in history.[2] As mentioned in Chapter 1, De La Torre is concerned with the hindering of liberation, finding that hope can be a source of oppression. He argues that the marginalized do not rebel because of the hopes imposed on them by dominant groups, and that these keep them from attaining their freedom. He articulates problems with hope in a Christian context, but there is no evidence of a counter-argument or alternative understanding of hope from other traditions or groups of thought; all hope is negated in the argument for *hopelessness*.

Though the broad claims around hope make the concluding arguments reductionist, in the book the author identifies material dangers in the concept of hope. As a way to delve deeper in understanding the principles of hope, I propose asking, "What are we hoping for?" and, "Where, or in whom, is our hope placed?" in order to reach a sustainable hope, not to blindly perpetuate it. I do not believe that hopelessness negates hope, just as doubt does not negate the existence of faith. The articulation of hopelessness in *Embracing Hopelessness* does not move the reader to a deeper understanding of hope and what could be the negative effects for the disenfranchised. Rather, such hopelessness seems to move toward despair and lack of imagination —as I will define later.

In the best of circumstances, lack of hope unsettles one's being and pushes us in search of new meaning. To despair, to succumb to desperation, clouds the imagination. De La Torre asks: "How can our Creator be so invisible during troubling times in which we live—times filled with unbearable life-denying trials and tribulations?"[3] This is one of theology's great questions and many, myself included, have asked it. However, although the book critiques Western scholarship and theological thought, the claims are rearticulated using the same "ivory tower" resources Western scholars use. If one looks for God in the same places that oppressive and contextually narrow Western and white supremist theology does, one will not find the God that infuses people with hope and elevates the disenfranchised. Speaking from the standpoint of my own practices as a researcher, I know that a handful of visits to *la frontera* and a couple of qualitative research interviews can give us only a glimpse of the Truth. Such cursory visits to another's world hardly justify universalizing claims.

True, De La Torre is concerned about the claims of salvation history and the justification of oppression and violence in search of meaning-making. He finds that hope reinforces oppressive structures and is not apparent among the oppressed; rather, he considers it to be imposed by the interpretation of those with privilege in order to expiate their guilt.[4] To this I argue that even salvation history is full of examples of sin, and that sin is—at its essence—Christianly unjustifiable. In other words, sinful acts cloaked by hope are not Christian hope. Or, as my mom would say, "*caridad contra caridad, no es caridad.*"[5] A hope that embraces, while denying, the existence of oppressive structures is a false hope, an illusion. But why should embracing hopelessness be the solution to negating an oppressive salvation history? De La Torre claims:

> For the world's disenfranchised to embrace a theology of hope, constructed independently of their real-life experiences, requires that they first deny their existential reality in exchange for the illusion of some dialectical movement toward a predominantly white utopia that continues to exclude them in the here-and-now. Better to remain with one's feet planted in solidarity with the marginalized, sharing their hopelessness, if we wish to contribute any praxis that might move beyond uplifting platitudes.[6]

Though the subject who needs to negate hope is used interchangeably, I agree that a theology of hope directed at people without considering their realities is dangerous and misleading. In the book there is an operative assumption where Christian hope does not exist beyond what the author recognized as hope—or, that is, because hope looked like white hegemonic Christianity, there was no hope arising from local and popular practices. A practical theology of liberation means engaging in empirical research on people's practices, as well as engaging in human interactions to seek out popular knowledge and wisdom. The approach I take in this book's qualitative research is *conocimento de base* (knowledge from the base).[7] Academic removal from *lo cotidiano* prevents us from honestly seeing the dichotomies and contradictions in which people live, making it easier to venture grand universal claims.

De La Torre and I are not as far from each other's commitments and groundings as the previous paragraph might suggest. But my embodied commitments and research findings bend toward hope, whereas in his work explains that hopelessness moves through desperation towards liberative practices. By contrast, I have found that in Puerto Rico, desperation has led to an increased suicide rate and a massive exodus towards Empire (the U.S.A.).[8] Without a hope that is sustainable—not a hope that is naïve—despair does not equate to collective, or even individual, liberation. If anything can mark the necessity of a sustainable hope, it is the imminent threat posed by humanity's unsustainable ways of life. By sustainable hope, I mean hope that can maintain the truths of people's social context and their trust in the Divine.

I agree with De La Torre that hopelessness embraces lament and that "to stand in solidarity is to stand in the space of the hopelessness they share."[9] So *what* moves us to stand in solidarity and endure with those who are lamenting the ills of their despair? Why should the reader embrace solidarity, especially one such as Ada María Isasi-Díaz describes? Solidarity, in her view, transcends mere agreement with others' commitments, citing the fact that one can walk away from being in solidarity. Solidarity is a commitment to mutuality that moves us towards resistance and liberation.[10] "Solidarity moves away from the false notion of disinterest, of doing for others in an altruistic fashion."[11]

In her work on solidarity, Isasi-Díaz draws on mutuality as solidarity in order to exemplify the dichotomy between oppressor and friend, understanding that people who walk with others in solidarity are not the same as those embodying the oppression. It is important to understand one's own space and place in this process of liberation-as-mutuality. Isasi-Díaz describes solidarity as a virtue and a way of life that is faithful to Christianity.[12] As theologians working in a field that directly engages with and in communities, and obligates us to engage people's lives, knowing where we stand in relationship to their struggles and their space is important for the sake of the community and the research.

At the end of his book, De La Torre does not try to force a hopeful response, which I appreciate.[13] Instead he proposes ethics for a *teología para joder*—a *"fuck it"* ethics.[14] People have different callings in the ways they participate in liberation; jamming the system is one of them. I do caution, however, that to jam the system without an aim or a thoughtful strategy can be detrimental for those with whom they are trying to stand in solidarity. It can also turn into a privileged attitude, since not everyone has the luxury of saying *"que se joda"*—"just fuck it." Whereas De La Torre categorizes hope as an illusion, I disagree, suggesting instead that illusion is the opposite of hope. That is why I not only articulate a discourse around hope but also highlight practices of hope that move toward liberation. Just as an illusion, a false hope, is unsustainable, so too one cannot live fully in desperation, despair, and with an ethics *para joder*.

One basic traditional understanding of Christian hope frames eschatology within a concern with resurrection and eternal life.[15] Certainly Christian eschatology is about hope, but eschatology is concerned with much more than death, heaven, and the end of things.[16] As De La Torre critiques this traditional understanding, so too do I search for an articulation of hope that takes into account not only the Christian imaginary of the afterlife but also the messiness of present life, in order to enliven a hope that is sustainable and driving toward life abundant. My aim is to articulate a Puerto Rican theology of hope that, while drawing upon a traditional understanding, is also complicated by the Puerto Rican context and practice. My articulation of hope in Puerto Rico is limited to the Christian understandings I found among my research collaborators, although the island and the Puerto Rican diaspora include many religious traditions. My goal is to understand how people in Puerto Rico ground themselves spiritually and socially in a hope that allows them to flourish and move forward in the midst of devastation and despair such as that caused most recently by Hurricane María and its aftermath.

Despair is not the opposite of hope. Despair is a state of being that creates a visceral response to the impact of one's hope being challenged and/or destroyed. Theologian Dominic Doyle defines despair as being without hope.[17] Along with Moltmann, he understands despair as a sin, because it shatters "the movement to share in God's goodness," and because he sees despair as focusing on the finite and rejecting participation in divine life.[18] However, labeling despair as sinful ignores the social conditions and, for some, the mental health issues, that lead to despair. Understanding despair as sin does not account for that which is out of our control, such as systemic injustices. Despair makes us reassess our hope, though because one cannot live sustainably in despair, desperation, or hopelessness, it is at best a temporary period of reassessment. De La Torre suggests we embrace desperation as part of hopelessness, believing that it often prompts people to seek justice.[19] But how can this be? The basis of our search for justice must be the hope that things can be different and just. It is true that "different" does not necessarily mean justice; it might be simply a temporary amelioration of conditions. But the move of desperation cannot be towards hopelessness but towards hope. In De La Torre's book, I would argue justice is the hope.

Despair, as I understand it, is not a sin —though it might lead to sinful acts— but a part of the human condition; it is a form of suffering. Understanding hope interchangeably with belief as a personal decision makes it easier to understand despair as a sin, with the individual as solely responsible.[20] But to hope, as I will explore, is an ontological category that people cannot simply decide to accept or reject. One can decide *in which object/subject* to place hope and *what to cultivate hope toward*, but one cannot decide on the *act* of hoping. The impulse of expectation through hope is part of our humanity, regardless of whether it is a good or a bad, a positive or a negative expectation. I am not currently adding value to hope, the value we add in social constructions. People might find a different articulation of a hope, but it is still hope. When there is true banishment of hope, life perishes. "*Donde hay vida hay esperanza*" (Eccl. 9:4): therefore, if there is no hope, there is no life.[21]

Optimism and Positivity

Optimism and positivity are not (necessarily) hope. There are other concepts that expand on the complexities of hope and help us better understand how hope is known and enacted. Optimism and positivity produce the certainty that what is wanted or desired will materialize in reality, whereas hope waits on the uncertain. The dangers of optimism, and its insistence on the desired outcome, is that it can make one unaware of the conditions and methods of its achievement. Laura Berlant observes that, "A relation of cruel optimism exists when something you desire is actually an obstacle for flourishing. . . . They become cruel only when the object that draws your attachment actively impedes the aim that brought you to it initially."[22] She sees optimism as "a scene of negotiated sustenance that makes life bearable as it presents itself ambivalently, unevenly, incoherently."[23] As the seemingly attainable good moves farther away, people develop ways to manage life moment to moment.[24] Berlant diagnoses the neoliberal crisis as the unsustainability of upward mobility and suggests that embracing optimism is a form of coping with this anxiety and crisis.

Although Berlant uses hope and optimism interchangeably in her work, optimism depends on what we can see and the trust we have set out in the system.[25] The optimist decides to put forward an attitude of certain expectancy that things will work out for the best. Hope, on the other hand, puts forward the possibility of the unknown. Hope is more magical (Alves), ontological (Anzaldúa), and flexible (Marshall).[26] Optimism also functions as the opposite of pessimism. They work hand in hand when, as a society or as individuals, we range ourselves along a spectrum between optimism and pessimism. Is the glass half full or half empty? Optimism, as a way of viewing the world, expects the best possible outcome. For example, hope tells me there is eternal life and resurrection. Optimism makes me believe that I personally will get to participate in this hope in its best form. Pessimism does not necessarily negate the hope, but as a stance, it makes me believe I will not participate in it.

Puerto Rican historian and sociologist Rafael Bernabe cautions his readers about optimism, especially easy optimism, and distinguishes it from hope.[27] Referring to the economic crisis in Puerto Rico, he argues: "*no tenemos mucha base para el optimismo, es cierto, pero la esperanza puede nutrirse del pesimismo . . . hay que buscar y hay que aferrarse a cualquier posibilidad de cambio.*"[28] According to Bernabe, the search for hope augments pessimism. He, however, believes that in order to find hope we need to organize pessimism. Like anthropologist Yarimar Bonilla finds in her work, "For dissapointment is always intimately bound with hope; dissapointment proves that apathy has not setteled in."[29] Bernabe's pessimism, as an organizing force, is not the same as De La Torre's hopelessness. Bernabe sees pessimism as the acknowledgement of that which is absent. Absence is a theme I will further explore with Rubem Alves as an important component of hope. Methodologically, my own search for what hope *is* and where hope *is* starts from negation. It begins from understanding what *it is not* conceptually and practically. It starts from the impossibilities of our social systems, from economic and spiritual scarcity; it is the unveiling of our illusions.

I understand illusion to be the opposite of hope; an illusory hope, a false hope, is like Berlant's cruel optimism. In our human need to be grounded and sustained, we hope. Sometimes these hopes are deceiving and cruel, or as Brazilian liberation theologian and educator Rubem Alves would call them, false prophets.[30] They become a distortion, an illusion both of hope and of the flourishing for which we are hoping. According to Alves, although illusions seem to be disconnected from reality, they are rooted in society's logic. He understands them as symptoms of concrete problems, created to make life bearable. One needs not only to destroy the illusions, but to ask what the social conditions are that have created the need for them.

For Alves, illusion also negates the pain the creative act entails.[31] Therefore, it looks for more immediate, soothing, and comfortable responses than the act of hope requires. Convincing oneself that the creative act toward freedom is not necessary is a false prophecy.[32] The illusion of the oppressor insists that the creative act is no longer necessary; the illusion of the oppressed, that creativity is no longer possible. Thus, they are joined in the same system.[33] "Illusions," Alves writes, "must be understood from *the way they function* and not from what *they say*. Instead of abolishing the real contradictions of social life through a creative act, they dissolve the ethical demand for it. By proclaiming the inevitability (or impossibility—either one) of the happy ending, they make it possible for business to go on as usual."[34] Humanity needs to become disillusioned in order to abolish what made the illusions necessary in the first place, for creativity is the child of hope.[35]

Maintaining the illusion, and eventually realizing its unsustainability, can quickly send us into despair. If people do not have resources to sustain themselves, —though not exclusively— people search for comfort, numbness, and expiation in order to ease the unsettledness of their despair. Central among such resources is community, the net that holds an individual or group in space and time when hope is lost and must be found again in order to live. The capitalist glorification of individualized upward mobility makes it more difficult both to develop communal hope and for individuals and communities alike to be held through a transition from hopelessness to hope. Womanist Monica Coleman laments the ways in which, as individuals, we do not "act as if we were interrelated."[36] Since evil and sin occur in a world that is relational, for Coleman, salvation, if it is to involve creative and not destructive transformation, needs to be articulated in relationship and community.[37] Hope, for the hopeless and desperate, is salvation/survival. A sustainable hope moving towards liberation and justice does not happen in a void or in solitude. A hope that can nurture community needs to happen in community within and from just relationships.

I have argued that in order to articulate a sustainable hope and develop a model for its cultivation, it is important to understand and bring into conversation the complexities of hope and its interrelated dimensions. I proceed now to discuss hope kinetically and in three dimensions: what is our hope, how does it manifest, and towards what it does it aim?

WHAT IS HOPE?

Hope Theology

In Spanish, the word "hope" conveys the action of waiting. The noun *esperanza* comes from the verb *esperar*, "to wait." *Una esperanza* is the thing for which I am waiting. Hope is not external though it implies expectation. It is often something active, but it can also denote passivity, since to wait can sometimes mean to hold still. Times of hopelessness are times when one grows weary from waiting, expecting.

As I continue to read diverse theologians with diverse foci (Moltmann, Marshall, and Caputo, among others), I see that people have never been exempt from feelings of hopelessness since in our worldly relations societies continue to have reasons for hopelessness. It seems that what prompted each of these authors to write was their perception that the world is continuing to struggle, and that humans have become increasingly hopeless, even nihilistic. In this work, my concern is the sense of collective social hopelessness specific to the island of Puerto Rico, which has caused multiple waves of mass exodus over the last century. Both those who stay and those who go experience hopelessness regardless of where they end up, coloniality both follows and remains.

In order to speak about hope in Puerto Rico, I have to take into account Christianity's role in the colonization of the island. How has a Christian colonial history affected the imagination of the people, and therefore the possibility of imagining hope? In particular, this colonial history has distanced the church and its message from both nonbelievers and believers. One example, the church's political advocacy against gender equity and queer sexualities has negatively affected many oppressed and marginalized people. Over time, both Catholic and Protestant Christian churches in Puerto Rico have developed a bad reputation in the public sphere because they have often failed to be "church," siding with those in political power and leaving the poor and vulnerable to suffer. Finally, I have to consider that the crisis in Puerto Rico is a material crisis, and that the church, because it has focused its public discourse on heavenly glory, is not seen as offering a viable solution for *this* world.

In such a context of crisis, the necessary theology of hope is one that awaits human flourishing. Movement from here to there needs to be accompanied by ecclesial practices that foster this flourishing in hopes of a fruitful future. It can be easier to have hope in an individual or as an individual than to engage in articulating a hope guided by the collective. Because it is invested in the community, human flourishing, within an ecclesial context, helps us build a systemic understanding and enactment of hope. Therefore, I propose a theology of hope that waits for (*esperanza*) human flourishing and exposes the ecclesial practices that enable it. Thinking this way helps us deal with the systematization of communal hope by understanding ourselves and our religious practices as more than individual. Practicing hope is a practice communal public witness.[38]

The upcoming sections briefly review the understandings of hope and the theology of hope in Jürgen Moltmann, Ellen Ott Marshall, and Rubem Alves. I highlight key concepts for my own theology of hope in the Puerto Rican context. As do I, these theologians are concerned with the impact of eschatologies and Christian hopes in the social sphere.

Jürgen Moltmann

Jürgen Moltmann has dedicated almost all of his scholarship to the study and articulation of a "hope theology." In *Theology of Hope*, Moltmann elaborates an understanding of hope through categorical descriptions of its components, including history, eschatology, and promise. He identifies the problems of modernity and its effects on Christian hope and spiritual life as they were displaced from public to private space through the lens of systematic theology. He aims "to show how theology can set out from hope and begin to consider its theme in an eschatological light."[39]

Moltmann's work is helpful in understanding the transcendence of Christian hope and its *telos*. He argues for hope as a way of looking at the future through Christ and the kingdom of God. He argues against romanticizing religion, because of its individualistic modern character, and against the romanticizing of hope as something unattainable. Moltmann speaks of eschatology in various categories, but all of them lead to an understanding of "that to which one looks forward in hope." He defines eschatology as the substance of Christianity, saying,[40] "The doctrine of the Christian hope, which embraces both the object hoped for and also the hope inspired by it . . . [For] Christianity is eschatology, is hope, forward looking and forward moving, and therefore also revolutionizing and transforming the present."[41]

Eschatology is the beginning of the promise, not its end. As philosopher Ernst Bloch would say, "True Genesis is not at the beginning but at the end."[42] Moltmann believes there can be no doctrine (*logos*) of eschatology because there can be no word for the "not yet." Christian eschatology cannot speak of the future as if it were "fortune telling"; rather, Christian eschatology departs from a definite reality and announces the future of that reality and its possibilities through the life and resurrection of Jesus.[43] Christian eschatology seeks to shed light on a reality that is coming and is rooted not in experiences but rather in the possibilities of that future. These possibilities are rooted in God's promises in the Scriptures: the promise of God's presence and God's kingdom.[44] For Moltmann, faith keeps us on the path of true life and is dependent on hope; hope reinvigorates faith and keeps us on that path.[45] The proclamation of the death of God comes out of "despair in the hope of resurrection," or more precisely out of the disconnection with God that leads to unfaithfulness and disbelief.[46] Believing in hope is what provides us with "inexhaustible resources for the creative inventive imagination of love."[47] His hope, tied to Jesus, provokes us to work with love.

Moltmann gives a clear picture of what is at stake in our world of increasing disbelief, and with the movement of Christianity and Christian hope into the private sphere and self-fulfillment. Against such a movement, Moltmann insists that Christ and Christianity are still the root of eschatological hope. Moltmann's work prompts me to ask about the practices that bring about hope, and to recognize those practices that articulate the resurrection, not of the individual at some unspecified moment in the future, but of communal life in the eschatological present. As he argues that our hope is to live *into* that resurrection of which Christ is the first fruits, maybe the living into tradition (a passing on of beliefs) and righteousness (the keeping of the promise) are the embodied practices that can lead people into living in this eschatological hope. However, this still leaves the question of how to interpret the promise and how to maintain the traditions that foster that journey of hope.

Moltman believes that hope has its foundation in suffering.[48] "A hope without contradiction is only a dream, a contradiction without hope is no more than, in Christian terms, rage."[49] He understands that hope is not an alienation of reality, but that reality should not be an impediment to hopefulness. This reality pushes against our hope, turning it to disbelief and becoming an impediment to hopefulness. But what happens when our disbelief is not a disbelief in God but in humanity? On the other hand, in the task of achieving creative action through faith, how can one teach/encourage an ideal of reality when people want to have a concrete floor to stand on and not an ideal one? Moltmann refers to crisis as our locus of historical analysis. I agree, and thinking about the current crisis in Puerto Rico, I would add that it is also the locus of theological analysis. If one sees the task of hoping as being about remaining *en la lucha*, as well as a task of understanding history's fluidity and openness, how does one address the issue of those who leave their situations due to hopelessness and despair? Though most immediately I am referring to people in Puerto Rico and/or leaving Puerto Rico, my question is not limited to this context since a people's oppression often results in exodus, as we see currently among people fleeing their homes in Central America, the Middle East, and Ukraine. In addition to that, if salvation and its work are through history (in flesh), then what is eternal life and how are we to understand spirit? Experience, as Moltmann states, should not define our hope. Nonetheless, our experience of God, or lack of it, does define our hope as mere mortals. Therefore, what are the heralds, the miracles, the beacons of hope that help us see and imagine the possibilities in our future? A lack of hope is also a lack of signs and revelation.

People's exodus in search of new hope in other countries is systemically rooted in the consequences of imperialistic practices. In the context of Puerto Rico, what does it look like to "go back" to a practice of religion not bound to Empire and its regulations? Moltmann argues against leaving the church to the state, for that tends to drown or suppress its revolutionary character.[50] However, in a context where the state has built an empire and subjugates people through the establishment of the Christian church, revolutionary action can quickly turn into an anti-Christian movement. What was/is wrong with religion is not the need/desire to connect to the Divine principle that guides and makes our humanity whole and communal, but our own "righteousness" and distorted practices of keeping that promise. Moltmann argues for opening ourselves and our hope to love.[51] He upholds love over justice and social order.[52] I wonder if he would consider justice and justice-making a component of love, for justice is not equivalent to retribution but can be an act of mercy, and thus an act of love.

Moltmann relies on Scripture and points toward God's promises to Israel. While it is true that the stories of God in the Scriptures let us see God's work in history and God's self in action (i.e., God's promise to Israel) through human experience, God's actions are not limited to those recorded in the Bible. The Christian canon may be closed, but not the revelation of God in space and time. An important character of hope is its inclusiveness and capacity for expansion, which Ellen Ott Marshall's writing can help us explore.

Ellen Ott Marshall

In *Though the Fig Tree Does Not Blossom*, ethicist Marshall, articulates a responsible and feminist Christian theology of hope. She defines hope as the "sense which generates and sustains moral agency" and argues that responsible hope unveils beauty and confronts tragedy.[53] In her feminist understanding of God's power and presence through relationality, she argues that to hope in God one must hope in humanity.[54] Similar to Coleman's argument from a postmodern Womanist perspective, mentioned previously, creative transformation and change happens within our relationality to all creation. As we continue to become community and refuse isolated decision-making by embracing more relationality, "we are constantly vulnerable to evil and also constantly capable of overcoming it."[55] Hope demands this wrestling with collectivity and expansion in order to move us forward towards flourishing and liberation.

One of the most valuable contributions I find in Marshall's work is her description of hope as *elastic*. Hope's disposition creates a dynamic (not necessarily balanced) within the tension of promise and peril, in order to be accountable to life's fragility and resilience. In other words, hope's tension keeps us grounded and elevated at the same time. Hope shapes the way one engages with the world and impacts our individual formation and affirmations.[56] The reason for hope's endurance is its elasticity; Marshall defines hope as a "dynamic positioning that accounts for its endurance."[57] The practice of hope, therefore, needs constant re-evaluation of its object and the means for its possibilities. She argues that if we focus solely on the object of our hope and not the process, we risk hurting the very thing we are hoping for.[58] For example, hope for economic stability alone, without considering the process to be set in place for its achievement, can hurt the hope for justice. A more concrete example is the government of Puerto Rico's plan to privatize natural resources to build resorts that employ locals without taking into account the long-term detrimental and irreversible environmental consequences.[59] In a situation of desperation, people can place their hope in unjust processes or persons because they need/want a quick response. Elasticity makes us aware of the possibilities and limitations. This happens as we consider the reality of our human condition and the history of consequences with the openness of promise and imagination in order to have a sustainable hope, or, for Marshall, a responsible hope.

I believe that a sustainable hope's challenge to despair is typically thwarted not by the apparent lack of God's intervention but by the consequences of our human interactions. To hope in humanity, as Marshall proposes, is a challenge all on its own. In the weeks after Hurricane María hit Puerto Rico, a long-time resident reflected, "These are the moments where we get to see the best and the worst of people; I hope the best prevails."[60] While some people were sharing their resources and cooking for their neighbors, others were stealing generators and looting stores. I then ask: How can the churches and Christian practices enliven hope in our fellow humans? Could understanding hope as elastic, as movement and shapeshifting, give us more space for grace and for the will to serve? The church continuously needs to reevaluate, outside the bounds of the colonial, what it means to practice radical love in order to exalt the best of our humanity; one can trust a humanity that loves and then hope for the best. To hope is not only to wait. Hope requires faith and trust. Therefore, how does the church carry the burden of hope? How does our humanity enliven our hopes?

This is where I find helpful Marshall's idea of hoping in pieces, because sometimes our hope gets fragmented. By understanding hope's elasticity and fragmentation, one can be released from the burden of despair. Marshall describes it thusly:

> Hope must be practiced because it is essential to daily life, the moral life, and the Christian life and because responsible hope does not come naturally. We must practice hope in order to cultivate it as a disposition. And, given the often overwhelming experiences of life, we must frequently practice hope in pieces, sometimes grieving and shouting, sometimes celebrating. The cumulative effect of such practices is a disposition that generates and sustains moral action because it attends to possibilities and to limitations. It buoys the spirit and steels the spine.[61]

To keep hoping, one needs to keep calling out evil and discerning hope that is illusion. By discerning our illusions, sometimes so intertwined with our hopes that fragmentation makes it hard to cultivate hope, one engages in hope's elastic movement. Moltmann argues that hope is not something you can see; to rely only on what we can see would restrict our imaginations. God calls us to "see" beyond the visible toward God's possibilities for a situation.[62] I partially agree, because if our hope depends on hoping in humanity from what we *see*, we are farther away from the kin-dom of God each day.[63]

However, one does need to *see* something, even if only in our imaginations, in order to persevere. By this I mean one needs to believe it is possible and envision it; one needs to identify indicators in history and human experience and in the Scriptures that remind them that these things are possible, and that hope in humanity is possible. With a hope that is elastic, one practices hope and recognizes that hope is a process. One cannot sacrifice how one hopes to achieve what is hoped for. People practice hope so long that it turns into a human disposition; this means that sometimes we have to practice hope in pieces. To practice hope in pieces means understanding the nature of hope and its contradictions when we do not always get/live into what we hope for. People hope not only by waiting but also by imagining and believing in the kin-dom to come, and that the kin-dom will come. I now turn again to Rubem Alves, who provides structural lenses for how to discern, on the one hand, our imagination, and, on the other, the impediments societal organizations impose on our hopes, rendering them not only illusory but impossible.

Rubem Alves

The late Brazilian theologian, educator, and psychoanalyst Rubem Alves is one of the fathers of Latin American liberation theology. In *Tomorrow's Child*, Alves argues for the disarticulation of "Organizations" and the birthing of a new society where the oppressed can live into the freedom they have imagined, and into that for which they have hoped.[64] He notes that our society is not only sick but designed to perpetuate that sickness.[65] It is absurd that humans have created a society where the goal is the apprehension and retention of power, and absurd conditions generate absurd responses. This, he says, is why there are dissenters in our societies, people who are often considered to be dysfunctional elements because they do not act according to the rules. The "Organization's" solution for the dissenters who become aware of their condition is to give more power to the already- oppressive and absurd system: "[A]dding power to the absurd one does not abolish it; on the contrary, it becomes still more hopelessly entangled in itself."[66]

Alves analogizes his society to the dinosaurs, whose extinction he claims was caused by "their arrogance of power."[67] He means that dinosaurs were too big for the structure in which they existed, and power cannot go beyond the logic of its generating structure. This arrogance entangled them in the "very absurdity of their organic structure," making it impossible for them to be able to respond to new challenges.[68] Likewise, power can become our god. Think of the mantra "the bigger, the better"; this is the value that controls the collective subconscious in many societies. Thus, one continues to enlarge society, meaning that society and individuals perpetuate the same faulty structures and methods, until society's demise under unsustainable "Organizations." Here, Alves is primarily critiquing the means and aims of production for the sake of profit and not for the sake of human life and the betterment of the human condition. In such a society, the end justifies the means when it comes to generating profits, as happiness is largely measured by our quantifiable productions.[69]

Alves declares our present way of production to be insane. The more power is fed into this insane system, the sicker and more dangerous it becomes until it reaches the point of destruction as our economy brings forward death to all creation through the exploitation of people and natural resources.[70] He offers, "We are trapped not for a lack of power, but by the unmatched effectiveness of our irrationality."[71] Our systems are not begotten by reason but are rationalized into existence and their persistence. The justification of our systems is not always informed by reason.[72] Here Alves cites scientific production as an example, noting that it has become an "exploitable function" because its economic perpetuation does not depend on scientists' desire for knowledge and innovation but on whomever is investing toward whatever purpose the investor intends.[73]

This rationalization is for the purpose of "Organization's" power, and in Organization there is no logic for life. Life is the means that fosters power as its *telos*.[74] However, life is an end in itself. Life is not there to reach something beyond it, but to exist abundantly as such.[75] Alves begins to unravel how acquiring power and control for the Organization is more effectively done through the repression of the imagination than through force and violence: "A slave must learn to love his master. He will then obey willingly. Values and thoughts can be made to coincide with those who dominate, and to obey the master will be just the same as being free. When that happens we see the act of domination as an expression of mercy."[76] Alves uses the example of the colony to illustrate. The colony has become an organ that has no will of its own but only does as it is told.

A major strategy for control of the imagination is the endless production of objects of desire that entice you to want the next thing and the next, always at a cost. Imagination cannot compete with the overwhelming rate of production and its enchantment when even emotional experiences become marketable.[77] When imagination is led to believe in an inevitable future, it becomes hopeless and purposeless. People adapt to this fate in order to avoid the pain that comes from realizing the pointlessness of their dreams.[78] We are then convinced there is no other option, and we are incapable of the "creative act" of imagining.

Alves notes that religious experiences as well as others (bodily, aesthetic, psychic, and mystical) are not commodities. Through them, humans are able to imagine other possibilities where sources of pleasure can be acquired at no monetary cost. These experiences can be attained without institutional control—in theory. They can, however, be dangerous as they can "conspire against the closed rationality of the system."[79] As imagination is labeled unrealistic and insane, we learn not to take it seriously.[80] Therefore imagination, magic, and religious beliefs can exist in the rationalization of the Organization as long as they are working for the Organization or are understood as unreasonable. Alves argues for a new body, a new beginning for our society, one that is built on new foundations, rather than for simply continuing our ways and making changes that further sustain the "dinosaur logic" that will extinguish us all. This new body that is wanting to be birthed will undoubtedly face rejection and be declared subversive by the old body. This is why hope is risky and subversive.[81] For this birthing to happen, society—the body—must become pregnant with hope.

Alves incorporates a third component into imagination and magic: play. In play, children are able to bend the rules of social norms at the will of their imaginations. Thus, play can create hope for freedom.[82] Imagination does not reveal a future, but mirrors the impossibilities of an impossible world.[83] Because "Organization" is good to the rich and powerful, they are committed to its continuity and preservation. This is why the imagination of a new future and its creative acts need to come from those who hope and suffer.[84] Solidarity is key for the envisioning of this new future. The way "Organization" works is through the "hope" of upward mobility. The end of our suffering comes when people change the location of their pain to pleasure, according to reality, using the organizing means already established in society. The obstacle or problem in this scenario is not the system but rather the individual's lack of ability to succeed, an example of cruel optimism.[85] Nonetheless, "the petty triumphs of the individual are no sign of hope to those who remain entrapped."[86]

How, in the midst of our entanglement with our organizing systems and the apparent impotence of getting out, do we find ways to foster a sustainable hope? According to Alves, society is not always ready for birthing but it can be ready for conception, especially in times of captivity.[87] Although I agree, I also wonder how to work both with the need for immediate responses in times of chaos, such as after Hurricane María, and with the patience that will also develop sustainable long-lasting solutions. Alves thinks the church is a space where patience and urgency can coexist. He sees Christian communal practices of hope taking shape as midwives of this new creation by being attentive to the small social indicators of the creative act. "Creation groans in travail. Already there is a new life and its womb, the source of our hope," that helps us endure.[88] Christian identity comes from the understanding that it is a teaser of the future: "It has visions of something that is as yet absent. And this which is absent is like a child slowly growing in the womb."[89]

Alves is not naïve about despair and the hopelessness that leaders and revolutionaries have to come to terms with. There are, however, those who decide not to give up. Why? How? Alves offers this suggestion:

> What is hope? It is a *presentiment* that *imagination is more real* and *reality less real than it looks*. It is the *hunch* that the overwhelming brutality of facts that

oppress and repress is not the last word. It is the *suspicion* that reality is much more complex than realism wants us to believe; that the frontiers of the possible are not determined by the limits of the actual, and that in a miraculous and unexpected way life is preparing the creative event which will open the way to freedom and resurrection.[90]

Alves uses the example of Jeremiah to talk about hope and captivity, as Jeremiah saw the possibilities of abundant life while still in exile in Babylon (Jeremiah 32). It is difficult to find the shape the creative act takes in captivity through our hope. Jeremiah understood it was not a time of exodus. Liberation cannot happen if the conditions are not created for it.[91] The theologian invites us to plant dates instead of pumpkins. Dates can take up to ten years to bear fruit, so it is likely the planters will not get to eat from the trees they planted. Pumpkins have a quicker return in production. Persecution for our hope will arise; however, "we must live by the love of what we will never see."[92] For theologian John D. Caputo, hope is either *"plenum"* or void. Hope is neither certain nor uncertain, but both an uncontainable promise and a threat; it is a risk.[93] Therefore, hope is uncertain not only because *nadie tiene a Dios echa'o al bolsillo* (no one has God in their pocket) but because we have to trust humanity.

Eschatology seeks to answer the uncertainty, and is often defined by interrogations of the end in order to understand new beginnings and/or fulfillments of promises. This understanding has also been aligned with hope. For Alves, a hopeful beginning is marked by the end of the "Organization," of those systems that hinder life. For example, traditional liberation theologies focus on the story of Exodus. My challenge from within the Puerto Rican context is not only that people's flight causes socioeconomic issues, but that they are fleeing towards the Empire as if it were the Promised Land. Can Puerto Rico be set in the framework of Exodus to speak eschatologically about hope and liberation? Here I find helpful Sergio Arce Martínez's focus on liberation and hope where he encourages society to rely on the ontological character of creation in the Divine.[94] The situation in Puerto Rico is an opportunity to create, but also (going further back) we can see it as an opportunity to create from nothingness and chaos. This is what Rubem Alves proposes in *Tomorrow's Child*: an eschatology that brings about liberation and the hope to work towards it. This hope requires trust in our humanity, revelation through imagination, and risk. "Eschatology," as Dermot Lane puts it, "is a protest against the premature closure of our understanding of the present and a plea for openness toward the future."[95] Alves's understanding of imagination, church practices, and social mobility are important components that more fully articulate an eschatological hope for Puerto Rico in its context.

WHERE IS THE HOPE?

Hope as Ontological

As a way of understanding why hope is so important for human flourishing and life's sustainability, I have suggested that hope is ontological, a part of the self, and that it is a category that precedes optimism, positivity, illusion, and so on. The main thinkers I engage with address a definition of hope as an impulse/action that generates from within. Ellen Ott Marshall defines hope as a generating *sense* and Rubem Alves as a *hunch* and a *presentiment*. Gloria Anzaldúa identifies this *sentido* (sense) as *la facultad*:

> *La facultad* is the capacity to see in surface phenomena the meaning of deeper realities, to see the deep structure below the surface. It is an instant "sensing," a quick perception arrived at without conscious reasoning. It is an acute awareness mediated by the part of the psyche that does not speak, that communicates in images and symbols which are the faces of feelings, that is, behind which feelings reside/hide. The one possessing this sensitivity is excruciatingly alive to the world.[96]

Our humanity is constantly struggling and in tension with the elasticity of hope, the expansion of imagination, and the revelation of our *facultades*.[97]

Hope also fits into the ontological Aristotelian categories of relation (we move towards hope), affection (being hopeful), and action (to hope).[98] This explains the complex elasticity of hope, why it is essential to our human experience as individual and relational beings with ourselves, society, and the divine as it interacts with different aspects of the self. What we *hope for* might be a choice, but *to hope* is an ontological practice. Everyone has *facultades*; not everyone cultivates them. Those who do embody hope more fully. "Hope," Caputo writes, "is a rose that blossoms unseen, blossoming because it blossoms, without why."[99] Hope is part of the self, though its strength and robustness is a matter of cultivation. Hope does not, necessarily, emote a bubbly-positive-optimistic-life's-cheerleader vibe. Hope *is* an integral part of our humanity, but how it manifests is conditioned by how we choose to practice it.

Hope as Practice

For hope to become a virtue, one has to cultivate and embody it. A virtue is the capacity to act for good. Theologian Colleen M. Griffith, speaking about hope, mentions the importance of the in-breaking of the Spirit as it positions us into action. Hope, therefore, is not a virtue just because we are capable of hoping. In order to position us into an action for good it needs to be guided by the Spirit. Hope becomes an action that impacts internal and external surroundings.[100] "To live by hope is to *practice hope* in the concrete and in the everyday, as a particular way of intending the future."[101]

Virtues are cultivated in practice; hope is cultivated in practice. For Marshall, hope empowers us to act; to practice a responsible hope, we need to pay attention to promise and peril.[102] "When in the face of tragedy we choose to act on behalf of the victim of history," she writes, "we affirm hope, forging a world more receptive to God's ever-saving presence."[103] For Alves, the Christian community imitates "the shape of hope" in the attempt to birth it and incarnate the pursuit of our values.[104] Hope is the dynamic behind it.

WHAT DOES HOPE LOOK LIKE?

Church Revival in Puerto Rico, 1933

Christian hope, its eschatology, is the realization of the kin-dom of God. For Moltmann it is the living memory of Jesus that guides the Church toward the hope of the kingdom through the Holy Spirit; there is hope because the Holy Spirit is present.[105] If the Holy Spirit is God's presence in the world, and was left to accompany us in our life/history's journey, then the freeing of the Spirit should move us toward liberation—hopefully! In the 1930s, during the time of the Great Depression and the devastation of Hurricane San Ciprián, there was a great awakening in the churches in Puerto Rico. People sometimes forget and do not see how the threads of history repeat.

In the 1930s the island had a considerably smaller debt than it does today, but fundamentally the same socioeconomic situation. People were immigrating to Hawaii and New York to work on plantations and in factories, and there were shortages of food and supplies as well as poor governance and infrastructure. The great awakening of the 1930s began with the work of local pastors.[106] This decade also marked a time when Puerto Rican intellectuals were strongly articulating a Puerto Rican identity and the independence movement was at its height. It was the beginning of the conception of a spiritually, economically, and socially hopeful future. The rest *is* history as the nails in the coffin of independence were hammered in 1952 when the island was declared *Estado Libre Asociado* (a Free Associated State, or Commonwealth) of the United States. The E.L.A. was understood as the realization of socio-political hope. Regardless of the greater magnitude of Puerto Rico's current situation, including the debt and its dependency history that it drags in its colonial DNA, this is not a new *cuento* (story). Since Hurricane María, the illusions of colonialism through "economic development" have been unveiled and people have begun to see more clearly how they function, as Alves argues.

The hope of Puerto Rican society, based on my experience and conversations, is the economic and cultural flourishing of the island. What does Christian hope have to say about this? Certainly, one can theorize and philosophize about hope without acknowledging its theological dimensions or a Christian interpretation. It will nonetheless be a disservice to understanding and exploring its depth and importance if not examined in the context of humanity's relationship with the divine. Hope reveals itself in practice when it moves outside the self, from that inkling and sense that something better and more just can be possible. The Christian Church's hope needs to reveal itself in practice; therefore, hope as a practice needs to manifest itself in public in order for it to be relevant and transform community.

In Puerto Rico after Hurricanes San Felipe (1928) and San Cipriano (1932), the church was able to arouse hope and a sense of a future among the people through a charismatic revival despite chaos, scarcity, and an exodus of much of the population to the United States. More recently, in 2017, Hurricane María likewise caused tremendous death, destruction, and trauma on the island. However, without making a generalizing claim, I have found instances where, with their long-practiced spirit of resilience, people in Puerto Rico once again have found ways of pushing through to hope and humor, and have "put on a good face." This conjunction with María has shed light on the ongoing systemic injustices, poverty, and colonial demise of the island. Showing humor here does not denote naïveté but resilience, a method of coping, much as hoping does not negate difficult and sometimes seemingly insurmountable realities. Here, smiling faces, good humor, or "putting on a good face" are not signs of disconnecting from reality in order to cope, but ways of facing it. It is a predisposition that challenges reality by not turning one's back on it. When channeled through the Divine, a smiling face is possible in the face of adversity because people can imagine other possibilities. Within Puerto Rican Christian history and practice there is a liberative hope that proves one can make *de tripas, corazones*—hearts out of guts.

CONCLUSION

Hope makes social demands.[107] The hope of the church needs to be informed by the hopes and pleas of the world. An example of the hope of the church meeting the hope of the world is the recent march of clergy and laypeople demanding that the Puerto Rican government audit the $72 billion debt. The US-appointed *Junta de Control Fiscal* is breaking off the island piece by piece to pay off this debt, affecting Puerto Rico's natural resources, education system, retirement funds and health care: anything and everything that serves as a vehicle to enact hope. *La Junta* and all it represents are killing hope for the sake of Empire. When church people partake in these struggles publicly, the hope for flourishing on behalf of the church and God's kin-dom meets the hopes of flourishing for the island. Hope moves us toward alternative systemic practices when enabled by the revelation of the Holy Spirit. Hardship will always be there (Mark 14:7); however, one is able to have a smiling face in the midst of it because hope sustains us through it. "Hope," as John Caputo writes, "is a spirit, the aspiration, the very respiration of God's spirit, of God's insistence, which groans to exist. Hope dares to say 'come,' dares to pray 'come,' to what it cannot see coming."[108] *A mal tiempo, buena cara*, confronts the situation, faces the storm. It is a disposition, as hoping can be a disposition, that challenges whatever lies ahead.

Chapter Three

About Practice: "A Buen Entendedor, Pocas Palabras Bastan"

The saying *a buen entendedor, pocas palabras bastan* means "for those who get it, few words are needed" or "a word to the wise is sufficient." It usually means that one can understand what is happening, or what needs to happen, and act without needing too many words. The last chapter presented a broad view of public participation, suggesting generally how the church, as an institution and body of people, can enact real hope. This chapter will present my qualitative research findings about practices of hope in the present situation in Puerto Rico, demonstrating in action what theory attempts to communicate. Here I argue that the work of the church in hope is the flourishing of humanity and creation, and I show how some churches in Puerto Rico embody this work. Rubem Alves argues:

> It is participation in a common universe of meaning that makes
>
> communication possible. *Community requires alliance of the spirit.*
>
> It cannot exist apart from the sense of ultimate commitment to a common future.
>
> And how beautiful it is when this discovery takes place! Words become unnecessary.[1]

The first section of this chapter presents resources for an ecclesiology that fosters liberation, flourishing, justice, and spirit. As an example of the materialization of hope in space and time, I present an overview of Puerto Rican churches' participation around political issues and ways those churches are present in the public sphere while seeking to influence the transformation of the social order. I initially frame and analyze this participation using Alberto

Melucci's social theory on collective movement, and provide an ecclesiological framework from, but not limited to, the work of theologians Letty Russell, Gustavo Gutiérrez, Leonardo Boff, and Jon Sobrino. The theme of individual participation and collective action runs throughout this book. I use it as a framework to continue developing a correlation between the work of the church and the hope that people in Puerto Rico hold on to. The Puerto Rican context adds a unique aspect to previous articulations of a theology of hope as it questions themes of colonization, coloniality, and disaster capitalism.

The second part of this chapter presents my analysis of the findings of my qualitative research. To begin glimpsing a possible materialization of hope, I researched Christian congregations in Puerto Rico that perform practices of hope and articulate a theology of hope in explicit ways. I chose the church not because hope cannot be found outside of church, but because I was curious about hope's relevancy and response in the face of major social upheaval.

My research included interviews with nineteen respondents from six congregations representing Christian denominations concentrated in the northeastern region of Puerto Rico: Christian Church (Disciples of Christ), Roman Catholic, Presbyterian Church in America, Baptist, Pentecostal, and an independent church. I knew access to these congregations would be challenging since my research plan was developed less than a month after Hurricane María hit the island on September 20, 2017. When I conducted the interviews five months after the hurricane, many sectors of the island still did not have electricity, water, or road access. Nonetheless, in the midst of the struggle of economic depression and scarcity, ostensibly draped in hopelessness, I found a spark of hope in people's everyday practices.

As mentioned in Chapter 1, for decades Puerto Ricans have experienced a strong sense of hopelessness in the face of continuous socioeconomic distress. As ethicist Melissa Pagán says: "Since Maria, these wounds [of colonization] have been put on full display before the world. They are a bitter reminder of our disposability, of how we do not matter."[2] Part of the inspiration I find in Rubem Alves, as previously mentioned, is his proposal about new beginnings that defy systemic limitations and expand our imaginations. In wondering how to move forward and imagining other ways of being in the world that foster liberation, I cannot help but reflect on death and endings. According to Johann Baptist Metz, Christian hope has an "apocalyptic sensibility." This sensibility moves the church to search for an answer about the future.[3]

To speak of embracing the apocalypse, the end, might be taken as a form of resignation. But to embrace an "apocalyptic sensibility" is to understand the human race as part of the cycles of nature (a nature we have exacerbated and disturbed). Against anthropocentricism, this explodes the illusion that we are the pinnacle of creation, and more so, helps us understand our relationality to others and nature, rather than focus on individuality. Death is a part of life and the problem is not death in itself, nor the end. The problem is the way we prematurely rush other humans and nature *toward* their ends, creating systems that sustain destructive patterns, and in our refusal to let them die as we continue to build and rebuild with the same decaying strategies and patterns.

The elimination of the human race is not the issue here; rather, it is how to prevent the most vulnerable and oppressed from continuing to suffer under the grip of those concerned with self-preservation, those that, for the sake of their own survival, rush the most vulnerable to their end. Apocalyptic hope is ultimately about the creation of a new reality. For Anzaldúa, "we revise reality by altering our consensual agreements about what is real, what is just and fair."[4] Of course, none of this is simple. However, there are glimpses of hope, flowers growing through the cracks of the concrete. My aim is to break down the concrete and see what is underneath. I invite you, through the analysis of collective liberative agency and ecclesial practices of hope, to begin imagining a new reality.

THE LOCAL CHURCH: INTERVIEWS

Every Puerto Rican, those away from as well as those on the island, suffered the devastation of María. In more ways than one, its aftermath leveled the island's inhabitants, because almost everyone was in the same situation: in need of supplies and primary necessities. It forced those who did not know their neighbors and their community to see eye to eye. It did not matter if people would normally have had the financial means to buy what they needed; there simply were no supplies or access to basic needs. Neither the local nor the external governments were ready for what was to come. It was churches, established community organizations, and the diaspora that managed to hold it together and make what was needed with what they had: *de tripas, corazones* (hearts out of guts).

I was already planning to include a field research component in my book, working with some of the over 6,200 Christian churches registered with the local Puerto Rican government.[5] As I was drafting the scope and breadth of the sample, Hurricane María hit the island. I quickly switched gears and selected congregations I knew had outreach programs in their surrounding communities both before and after the hurricane. Not knowing when travel to the island, electricity, and access to roads would be restored, I also selected these churches based on physical accessibility and the possibility of telephone/email communication with pastors. For the purpose of keeping my individual collaborators' identities confidential, I will be presenting data drawn from at least three common responses to my questions, rather than highlighting the particularities of each individual. I will only be using the name of congregations or speaking about a congregation as a whole, for example, to highlight its programming (which is public information). If I need to speak about a particular collaborator, I will use them/they/their pronouns and refer to them by a consistent number ("Collaborator #16").

I conducted the interviews from March 15, 2018, to April 2, 2018. These were the last two weeks of Lent, as well as the time when the island went through a critical revision of the work reform.[6] The work reform proposed by *La Junta* in March 2018 imposed a reduction of vacation and sick days and allowed for unjustified and unpaid layoffs, amongst other things. This reform did not pass, but its prospect created a crisis among workers in the island, including the fear of a much faster emigration rate. I met my collaborators at their local churches, their homes, or at a restaurant. I attended the main worship service at each local congregation: five held on Sunday morning and one held Sunday night. I also read the congregations' online material, pamphlets, press releases, and other content in the public domain.

The selected churches, all from the northeast part of the island most readily accessible in the aftermath of María, were: Iglesia de Dios Misión Internacional in Río Piedras, San Juan (Pentecostal), Iglesia San Francisco de Asís in Old San Juan (Catholic), Mar Azul in Guaynabo (Independent), Iglesia Cristiana (Discípulos de Cristo) in Fajardo (Disciples of Christ), La Travesía in Guaynabo (Presbyterian Church in America), and Primera Iglesia Bautista in Carolina (Baptist). The memberships of these congregations varied from fifty to five hundred members. I interviewed the senior pastor and at least two leaders (ordained and non-ordained) from each congregation for a total of nineteen interviews.[7] I interviewed eleven men and eight women. Eleven, including nine men and two women, were ordained. They ranged from twenty-seven to sixty-six years of age with a median of fifty-one.[8] Seventeen interviews were conducted in Spanish and two in English.

Those I spoke with self-identified as having conservative (nine) and moderate (eleven) theologies. Interestingly, most of my interviewees struggled with this identification for one of three main reasons. First, they usually began by making a distinction between what these terms meant in the United States in contrast to Puerto Rico. Two, they distinguished between the dogma and doctrine of their congregation and that of other congregations. Three, their understandings of the question were explicitly or implicitly conditioned by their desire to know if I was asking about LGBTQAI matters or politically aligned ideologies. Although all of these congregations and their denominations are against gay marriage and/or consider queer sexuality and nonbinary people sinful, some of my collaborators wanted to understand these theologies more deeply and questioned their church's response towards queer people. Though questions on LGBTQAI issues were not part of my standard interview, people usually spontaneously referred to local controversies around this population, especially when asked about the importance of the church's public participation.

Although nationality was not one of my criteria for selection and sample balance, collaborators self-identified along a spectrum of nationalities as Puerto Rican, Cuban, Mexican American, and American, giving an idea of the diversity one typically finds in Puerto Rico. Related to this point, all the collaborating churches have been impacted by ongoing outmigration, even before the hurricane, and they have had to develop strategies for coping with loss and empowering both those who leave as well as those who stay. In a congregation of fewer than one hundred members, one family per month might leave for the United States. The collaborators were concerned about the organization and sustainability of practices of hope and justice that bring forward creation's flourishing at a time when the community is bleeding through migration.

My interview questions focused on my collaborators' perception of the church and its relationship to Puerto Rican society. I wanted to understand the congregation and the individual's understanding of hope, and whether their hope (whether or not that included any explicitly theological or transcendent dimensions) correlated with their material hope for society. Although the members of all these congregations belonged to every social class, my collaborators themselves ranged from lower-middle-class to middle-class.[9] I have divided the data into three sections. First, I discuss their practices, including some of the particularities of each congregation, their location, and their work in communities. Second, I discuss their hopes: I outline their definitions and understandings of what hope is and where they place their hope. Third, I describe the desired outcome of their hopes, their *telos*.

Practices

In the process of working with María's aftermath, these local Christian churches acknowledged the intentionality and new-found purpose of collaborative interdenominational work. All of them were disappointed at the lack of response, preparation, and compassion of local and US authorities. They were surprised by the poor ecumenical work the churches in Puerto Rico had managed to get away with up to the present.[10] Because of this history, they were concerned that once everything is restored these new practices of communal engagement and collaboration will diminish or cease. But in the process of hurricane response, they also realized and continued affirming that the church is *la gente* (the people) and its work is its service to them and all of creation. In this section, I present a brief description of each congregation and its predominant outreach programs. These descriptions are a conglomerate of the collaborators' stories about their congregations.

Iglesia de Dios Misión Internacional in Río Piedras is a Pentecostal church in the town of San Juan. It was founded in 1928 after Hurricane Felipe's devastation, only five years before the major Puerto Rican revival of 1933. This congregation emphasizes the experience of the Holy Spirit's baptism and from the beginning paid close attention to the area's marginalized communities. Its members are ethnically diverse; other than Puerto Ricans, Dominicans are its biggest population. In terms of social class, the congregation ranges from diverse economic scales. Its three predominant outreach programs are its evangelistic ministry, its work with poor communities, and the support of its own congregants with poor financial resources and legal status in the island. This congregation has also been undergoing one rapid theological shift. Up until María, based on my experience and that of the project collaborators, Puerto Rican popular religious discourse often referred to natural disasters and their aftermath as godly punishments rather than as consequences of its geographical positioning. Churches like the M.I. in Río Piedras, or the Baptist church in Carolina, that have begun teaching their congregants about ecological change and about how to be prepared for natural disaster have seen how people's anxieties are reduced since they were able to stop correlating natural disasters with Godly punishments and were given help to prepare for them.

Iglesia San Francisco de Asís in Old San Juan is a Catholic church founded in 1876 and administered by the Capuchin order. Lay members mentioned in several instances that they were *enamorados* (in love) with the order because it lives out the Gospel through its service to and compassion for the homeless population of Old San Juan. Because of its location in a historic area, the congregation is transient. Roughly fifty people are regular members of this church, but most of its attendees are one-time visitors. Despite this apparent instability, San Francisco de Asís has a robust ministry of aid and care for the homeless through the nonprofit *Hogar Padre Vernard*. The ministry bathes, clothes, and feeds the homeless, who know that this is their church and safe haven, though they do not all participate in worship. My collaborators spoke about the importance of bringing hope to the people through the joy of the Gospel, and how they practice that hope in the love they pour into their service. They care for the rehabilitation of their community, providing services and counseling toward this aim, a job that proved arduous—but not impossible—after María.

Mar Azul is an independent church in the town of Guaynabo. Founded in 2010, this congregation tries to create community with the unchurched, mainly people who have been hurt by more conservative traditions or are skeptical about religious life and Christianity. The congregation says it is guided by principles, not by traditions. Members are predominantly young people and young families. When the congregation established itself and needed to choose a name, its members wanted to come up with one that had no association with any tradition but signified something everyone could have in common: Puerto Rico. The name they chose translates to "blue ocean." Mar Azul is located in a relatively affluent community and rents its space from an Anglo congregation that owns the building. Interestingly enough, members of the congregation do not live in the area but come from other, adjacent parts of the town.

Mar Azul stands out for the expansion of its labor in the aftermath of María. Many of its congregants, despite the situation, decided to stay on the island because of the community they experienced in this church. Having cultivated the topic of hope and service for months before the hurricane, this congregation went quickly into action. They established a distribution center where they took hundreds of FEMA's rotten boxes, dug in, and salvaged whatever was edible to distribute to the communities. Their actions were accompanied by deep theological reflection at every step. They also began running an operation of small missions as churches in the United States began to reach out to channel resources and help through them. As the state of emergency ramped down, they decided to adopt two communities and establish a five-year rebuilding plan. They have gone through training and have done intentional work to avoid the paternalistic tendencies of missions, seeking to help these communities where they want to be helped and integrating the congregation into the community to form a bigger, stronger whole.[11]

Iglesia Cristiana (Discípulos de Cristo) in Fajardo, a Disciples of Christ congregation established in 1999, was the result of a merger between a Disciples of Christ children's ministry and a small bible-study group led by a Pentecostal pastor, giving this congregation a neo-Pentecostal touch. They described its members as predominantly middle-class and lower-middle-class; it is located in a predominantly lower-middle-class to working-poor community. The congregation believes that service is the church's responsibility. Before María they had been running a lunch program for homeless people and had an American Sign Language (ASL) program well underway. After María they reshaped their mission and aim. A day after the hurricane, the congregation's pastor drove house to house to account for its members and list their needs. The denomination provided much aid to its local congregations, including electric generators, becoming a source of power for the nearby communities. Loan forgiveness, pension advancements, and other forms of financial support from the denomination at large allowed the Fajardo congregation to share its resources with other congregations and smaller nondenominational neighboring churches.

After the demolition of many of the structures in Fajardo and the rest of the island, what remained strong were the already-established communitarian bonds that allowed other bonds to form and expand. Many church members did not have access to food and water and there was no electricity. On Sundays Iglesia Cristiana began offering free lunch, which for many of its congregants made the difference between going to church or not due to the laborious task of cooking with no power and the use of gasoline to get to worship.

Because of their previous work with disabled people, congregants were able to help members of this population connect to local agencies and to be aware of what was happening. Communication was a challenge through the first stages of the aftermath. The congregation learned how to work without fear in the face of economic limitations, giving from what they had—a lesson shared by many of the other congregations I studied, where congregants needed to learn and trust that if they gave, they would still have enough for themselves. Because of the economic depression that followed María, this church of 115 members lost twenty-three to migration to the United States in 2017. Citing Habakkuk 3, however, one of my interviewees described a revival during the past year; despite the lack of members, the people who stayed and showed up were hungry for service. Whereas in the past there had been a decrease in leadership, now they have leaders to spare.

La Travesía in Guaynabo is one of two Presbyterian Church in America congregations in Puerto Rico. The other congregation is the Anglo Trinity Church, a daughter congregation of La Travesía. Collaborators from this congregation understood La Travesía as a contemplative church for young unchurched people. It started as a Bible study in 2011 and grew into what it is today. Its membership is predominantly young families and young working adults who, according to the pastor, range from middle-class to upper-middle-class. In the hurricane's aftermath, the pastors incorporated lament into their worship services, understanding that—as they said—being sad together is an act of faith. Because this community had already been cultivating familial bonds and its ethos is religious education, in the aftermath of María the congregation realized it needed to respond to the call of service to those outside the community if members wanted to truly practice what they preached.

As they began to offer assistance in the communities, their operation and mission grew, and they organized systematically to create sustainable forms of aid so efforts would not be reduced once "things went back to normal." They began harvesting what they had sowed while building partnering networks.[12] One of the significant results of María was the unveiling of the island's existing poverty; they did not want this to continue to be the norm. La Travesía established a collective of churches that also had the mission of serving their neighboring communities. Christ Collaborative includes Iglesia Wesleyana in Guaynabo, Iglesia Catacumbas in Camuy, Mar Azul (already discussed), Alianza Cristiana y Misionera in Vega Baja, and Iglesia Cristiana (Disciples of Christ) in Santa Rosa. They organized workshops to learn and teach how to sustain these relief efforts, and how to work with short-term missions coming from all over the world. Pastors from all over the island and from many denominations attended these workshops. Like Mar Azul, La Travesía created an online portal to connect with Hurricane María relief donors and volunteers. They have also adopted a community, committing to a five-year collaboration with the community's local pastors and members.

Primera Iglesia Bautista in Carolina is a Baptist congregation founded in 1901. Its mission includes evangelization through service, and they take a holistic approach to ministry. The congregation's motto is *"una iglesia que adora a Dios y sirve al prójimo"* ("a church that loves God and serves its neighbors"). Its members vary across social class and ages, but their largest age group is older than fifty-five, as their younger population has been migrating to the United States. This congregation is very well known locally. It owns a school, a library, radio programs, a retirement center, and a social services foundation, among other large projects such as a food pantry and clothing warehouse, all always in service of the community and the expansion of the Gospel of Jesus.

The congregation is known, however, not only for its big endeavors, but because of its commitment and perseverance in neighboring communities where ministries have lasted for years. In the aftermath of María members of the congregation began the practice of walking through the neighborhood at night, praying and interceding for it. They also went house by house, asking people directly for what they needed, in a project they called "The New Jerusalem." They said they prioritize ministering with compassion and believe the cornerstone of their practices is prayer. On their altar, a banner reads *"oramos por Puerto Rico"* ("we pray for Puerto Rico").

GOD, CHURCH, AND PARTICIPATION IN SOCIAL MOVEMENTS

The research focuses on the shape and dynamic of hope even in the midst of hopelessness. The interviews I discuss later in this chapter are aimed at detecting whether the discourse around hope in Puerto Rican churches is consistent with their practices. In recent decades, many churches and religiously affiliated people in Puerto Rico have taken public stands in protest against unjust political and economic developments (although I do not imply that there was no public stance before this period). Among several recent examples, people in the town of Vieques had been suffering from cancer and were evicted from their lands for decades due to the military training site located on Puerto Rico's smaller island. The withdrawal of the US Navy and Marines between 2001 and 2003 came after long years of fighting and litigation by activists, clergy, artists, and politicians. Many clergy and laypeople, moved by their faith to search for justice, have been arrested for civil disobedience.[13] In 2014 a Methodist Bishop, Rafael Moreno, organized a protest against the implementation of a new tax, the I.V.U.[14] Also in 2014, the Puerto Rico Council of Churches and the Interreligious and Ecumenical Coalition supported the release of political prisoner Oscar López Rivera.[15] On Good Friday 2018, Catholic priest Pedro Ortiz and the group *Todos Somos Pueblo* organized a protest in front of the offices of *La Junta de Control Fiscal* to denounce the aggressions of the government against the *pueblo* as sinful. They used a purple banner reading "*Que la crucifixión del Pueblo no nos sea indiferente.*"[16] These various actions undertaken by Christians in Puerto Rico can be interpreted through the eyes of Rubem Alves, who argues that to protest or to demonstrate against social injustice can become futile if it is not accompanied by acts of resistance.[17] This is why social movements are so important. They go beyond words and attempt to sustain social change.

Social Movement Theory

Alberto Melucci, an Italian sociologist focusing on social movements and collective action, writes in his book *Challenging Codes: Collective Action in the Information Age* that social movements are not entities unified by one ideology but that they are systems of action.[18] Movements tend to be homogenized by their guiding struggle or ideology and they get so wrapped up in the details of political controversy that we do not pay attention to these systems of action surrounding and feeding the epicenter of the conflict. In trying to address questions of change and hope in the Puerto Rican context, one has to understand the intersectionalities of all the actors and factors in community organizing and collective action, as well as how they shape, move, and jam these initiatives. Melucci questions the lack of attention by social movements to systemic issues that are at the heart of the problem and that, if left unaddressed, end up getting dragged into new social problems and new social movements.[19]

This is also one of Rubem Alves's critiques, and why he argues that we need an entirely new system. We continue to repeat our struggles because of a lack of depth in analyzing these underlying and surrounding conflicts. For example, the toll of capitalism is dragged into "new issues," now in the shape of neocolonialism and neocapitalism, because we never solved it in the first place. Melucci believes a society that has built-in space for the thrust of movements can accommodate the complexity of these conflicts as well as make sure they are not minimalized or flattened out.[20] Social movements tie in contradictions and conflicts because they are placed at the intersection of structure and change.[21] Puerto Rico's contemporary history provides a great example to focus on and analyze the tendencies of social movements to repeat the same oppressive capitalistic systems that created the original problem. Melucci's argument about movements' capability to make room for complexities, I believe, is an important growing edge for Christian churches in Puerto Rico, which often reach impasses due to a lack of room for diverse leaders and discourses.

Another helpful aspect of Melucci's argument is his notion that collective processes are either a result of the disintegration of the system or of a transformation of the structural basis of that system.[22] Here lies an important aspect of the conflicts in Puerto Rico: wanting the disintegration of the system without realizing that what one needs is a transformation of the structural basis. A long history of colonialism, paternalism, capitalistic advantages, and oppressive theologies create the struggles of today. Without addressing how these play out in society, social movements will continue to march and protest in circles.

The Workers' Movement in Puerto Rico

A good example for understanding the development and struggles of community organizing in Puerto Rico is the history of the workers' movements and the *lucha de clase* (class struggle). That history of social organizing sheds light on current social movements and the island's present imaginary about organizing. Workers began to organize in Puerto Rico at the end of the nineteenth century. One of the few things that the 1868 *Grito de Lares* revolt was able to accomplish was a more autonomous and organized workforce. Before the United States invasion in 1898 there was already a system in place for *artesanos* (artisans) that continued to develop afterwards. Historian Gervasio García describes the first decades of organizing as *organización solidaria* (organization in solidarity).[23] The workers had cooperatives and a system to cover for each other in case of injuries, and they even began moving next to each other and forming communities. New practices of *compadrazgo* (godfathering) began developing.[24] It had been common practice to ask the landowner or someone in a higher position to baptize one's children. Now *artesanos* were asking their colleagues, bypassing the upper class and relying on equals to develop networks and familial ties.

As US law began to overtake existing law in Puerto Rico, however, solidarity and collective action turned into individual progress and upward mobility.[25] As mentioned in the first chapter, at the start of the United States' presence on the island there was not a strong sense of national identity because there was nothing opposing it. With the local government incentivizing people to immigrate to the States, and fear of the Independence party impeding any advancement of the island's assimilation of US culture and government, the spirit of class struggle started to diminish; even access to education enabled this because it was a means for upward mobility without *lucha de clase* (class struggle).[26] This gave rise to an increase of economic struggle and to a socialist party. With the continuous development of an industrial economy, as well as the conflicts that developed between Puerto Rican and US laws, solidarity began to dissolve, especially in light of government programs shipping workers to the States. Individual upward mobility became a means for dissolving practices of solidarity.[27]

The fact that there were options (immigration and education) for economic flourishing does not mean that these were the only social movements in Puerto Rico. After the diminishment of the Workers' Movement, there have been several related to, for example, housing justice, the military presence on Vieques island, the liberation of political prisoners, noninclusive legislation, and financial justice.[28]

The collective interrelated weight of colonialism and capitalism drowns any efforts at systemic social change. For example, the current resistance to education on gender equality is directly linked to a loud and powerful religious fundamentalist culture that permeates the governance structure, which is not simply resolved by evoking the principle of the separation of church and state.[29] Aside from fundamentalist influence in politics, views against gender equality are deeply embedded in the country's politicians; the state, after all, is made up of subjects, not objects. To offer another example, the problem with financial justice is directly linked to a perpetual colonial and dependent status that runs deeply into the lack of a sense of self-governance in the country.

Collective action in Puerto Rico tends to hit a wall when faced with the legal limits of its autonomy in relation to the United States, truncating its potential progress. This is not a relationship of equals. While the layers of control have varied over time, there have always been several such layers above Puerto Rican legal "sovereignty." At one point in Puerto Rican history, the US Federal Court of Appeals could overthrow any decision the Puerto Rico Supreme Court made. Puerto Rico is currently under the supervision of *La Junta de Control Fiscal*. Meanwhile, internal conflict over the political future of the island (commonwealth vs. statehood vs. independence) clouds and frustrates any conversation that tries to address political issues and conflicts.

In the 2012 volume *Trabajo Comunitario y Descolonización*, a group of sociologists and social workers from the University of Puerto Rico developed a model of community organizing that pushes for the decolonization of the island as a key component for solving discontent in Puerto Rican society. Interestingly, the authors emphasize the philosophy of liberation as a critical lens on history and against concepts of Eurocentrism and U.S.A. superiority.[30]

For this group of scholars, "community" is a process of liberation where persons achieve a sense of belonging, develop an identity, and engage in social integration and full political participation. They argue for a dialectical practice between an individual's recognition of citizenship and participation in political structures through a process of conscientization.[31] This process gives citizens the opportunity of becoming political agents with the capability of changing their realities and the relationships of power in society.[32]

The authors of *Trabajo Comunitario y Descolonización* regard decolonization as an ethical political matter. I would argue it also needs to be a theological matter. It is interesting that they see pessimism as such a constant tendency that even when proposals are good and well thought out, people divest. We are forced to ask where this automatic mentality of defeat comes from—an especially crucial question when one wants to develop a theology of hope! Their model argues for a nonpartisan approach; however, to speak about decolonization automatically moves people towards the assumption or insinuation of political independence.

Their project seeks a nonpartisan community movement of common citizens that assumes the collective responsibility for society's transformation. Without being overly pessimistic, my experience has been that liberation and independence are often polarizing concepts and too charged to be practical for organization. These concepts are often interpreted as separation from the United States, a notion that strikes fear in many Puerto Ricans. Unless one is speaking to a specific group that understands the coloniality of power (and usually these are not the ones who need mobilization), many people are terrified of independence. Language and framing are very important if organizers want to speak to the masses.

The *Trabajo Comunitario y Descolonización* authors also recognize that they are writing from and for an academic audience. How are we to bridge participation of all the actors needed to enact social change if there is a gap of communication and access between groups? Melucci claims that the oppressed are not usually the ones who participate in movements first. He also says that new movements are born out of preexisting relationships, and Saul Alinsky bets on this being true as well.[33] The challenge is that the rhetoric used to appeal to people who are directly affected by an issue, and active practices of coming together, may tend to be restricted to academic spaces and spaces dominated by those with education or from higher economic classes, who then end up staying there. The model proposed in *Trabajo Comunitario y Descolonización* establishes its goals and objectives for decolonialization within a philosophical framework of liberation and critical humanism, relying on theoretical concepts of social construction, citizenship, and a dialectic with historical materialism.[34]

This model sheds light on the potential struggles and challenges people in Puerto Rico face when organizing. At this point, Saul Alinsky's *Rules for Radicals* may be helpful in understanding the materializing of movements. Alinsky proposes the use of structured organizations and the creation of symbols to get people to mobilize against a common enemy.[35] All of the Puerto Rican authors I have encountered agree that successful social movements on the island need to be nonpartisan, engage in cross-ideological solidarity, and participate in popular education. However, combining these insights with Alinsky's proposal to partner with an already-organized structure means that this organized structure needs to engage in changes from within before mobilizing outwards in order to meet the requirements of being nonpartisan and inclusive.

I am, of course, thinking about a very specific structure: the church. Alinsky wants "radicals" to work within a pre-organized structure to prevent having to start from scratch, but if the church in Puerto Rico wishes to engage in just political action, it needs to work through the issues that impede it from having a successful public participation in the first place: religious colonialism, harmful fundamentalist views (for example against LGBTQAI rights), and economic power (e.g., if the mobilization is against something in which an individual church member or religious group has a financial investment).

Hence, what is important about social movements for articulating a theology of hope? For starters, it is knowing that one is working with the world as it is, not with its ideal. Although the church in Puerto Rico has pioneered many initiatives in community organizing (some positive, some detrimental), the ones that have been more unifying and fruitful in achieving their goals have been the ones where the church participates with other coalitions. *La iglesia no siempre va a llevar la voz cantante*, and that is fine.[36] Community organizing is always in motion; it is difficult to accurately track or even move in the same direction all of the time.

A Spanish proverb says that *Jesús era manso, pero no menso* (Jesus was docile but not dumb). Perhaps this is too idealistic, but if we speak about *evils* then maybe we can keep in mind the humanity of our enemies and work to exorcise the evil rather than the person, even as specific people must still be held accountable for the evil that they do. This is an important tension. But, as previously noted, Melucci says that a society built to contain the tension of collective action is a society that can hold its contradictions and move towards change without minimalizing or flattening its complexities. Holding a human enemy in these tensions of docility and savviness helps us develop the movement further because it forces us to complexify our imagination.

Social movements are important for articulating a theology of hope because they enact hope, embodying the possibility of hope becoming a reality. One can only imagine what a decolonized church looks like in Puerto

Rico, but it is still important to know the systems of actions that are at play or built-in. Such knowledge is part of the process of conscientization with the hope of liberation. Gloria Anzaldúa wondered what would happen if she tried to find a pure version of herself; she narrates how she started stripping parts of herself until there was nothing.[37] Coming to terms with the systems that influence who one is eventually helps that person in society. Hopefully this knowledge moves us into searching for better ways to be in the world, to make new life in spite of what shapes us. Maybe when the church learns to strip itself of coloniality, instead of nothingness it will find itself rendered naked and returning to paradise.

Paz para Vieques

An example of a social movement articulating a theology of hope in Puerto Rico is the activist campaign on *Paz para Vieques* (Peace for Vieques). I had been marching for *Paz para Vieques* with my parents ever since I can remember. The movement was a struggle against the US Navy's presence in the town of Vieques that went on for over seventy years, reaching its peak in the early 2000s. The military finally left the island in 2003. Roberto Vélez writes about how the history of Vieques and its struggle became a mnemonic device that shook and mobilized Puerto Ricans into action.[38] He believes that "the articulation of a mnemonic model in narrative analysis of mobilization, stresses the significance of the cultural processes and their centrality in transition from cognitive liberation to massive mobilization."[39] For years the struggle had only been regarded as "political" and anti-United States; hence, with very rare exceptions only *viequenses* and socialists participated. It was not until 1999, when a civilian was killed in a bombing simulation exercise (many people had already died of cancer and natural resources had been destroyed), that the island's righteous indignation and massive mobilization kicked in. Then those seventy years of history became part of the *pueblo puertorriqueño*'s history, on and off the island. Civil disobedience by ministers, priests, artists, social activists, and students became a common act of resistance.

Paz para Vieques is the paradigmatic Puerto Rican social movement: colonial struggle, political struggle, popular action, and public theology wrapped in one. In the midst of the hype, a collective of musicians got together to write a song to gather support from Latin American countries. I remember the day of the video's debut on the news. All our neighbors gathered to watch it at our home. The lyrics describe drowning the sounds of bombing with psalms, how dreams are broken and heaven is made smaller, how all of the truths came together, how the *viequenses'* voice grew with the people's voice; because of love for the same things, we have each other in song. The location of hope in collective movements is the resistance of *el pueblo*. It is *el pueblo* that has the language of hope in its practices. The institutional church in Puerto Rico needs to open itself, get on board, and work with what it has towards the struggle for justice and creation's flourishing.

ECCLESIOLOGY AND THE PUBLIC SPACE

Before moving on to an analysis of ecclesial practice and hope in Puerto Rico following Hurricane María, it is necessary to establish some theoretical benchmarks against which to test those practices. I borrow from Gustavo Gutiérrez, who argues that the church is not an end to itself; just because the clerical structure and physical structure of a church (in his case the Catholic church) exist does not mean that the church's mission ends there, nor that what we are seeing *is* church.[40] He believes the church needs to be evangelized by the world, thus establishing an important claim about the church's relationship to the world. This does not imply the church has nothing to say to the world; rather, it suggests that if the church does not let the world in, it becomes irrelevant.

My approach to analyzing ecclesial practices, like that of Gutiérrez, involves this dialectical process between the church and the world. As a result, I understand "church" in a particular way. The actual institution of the church is *from* this world. Therefore, to speak about church and world as opposites seems like an oxymoron. In John 17:15, Jesus says to the Father: "I do not ask you to take them out of this world but to deliver them from evil." With this in mind, I understand the church that is in dialectical relationship with the world is the one that reaches out to understand and live into what is not of this world as it seeks deliverance from evil.

This framework for thinking about church and world relies further upon other key theologians and ecclesiologists who approach the topic from liberationist, postcolonial, and decolonizing perspectives. According to theologian Jon Sobrino, God is where the poor people are; for Cláudio Carvalhaes, God is where those excreted from society live.[41] A Christ-like church that focuses on the God of life for the marginalized and oppressed is founded in liberation, social change, and revolution. With this in mind, I seek ecclesiological themes of social change, revolution, and liberation that will contribute to a sustainable hope. Four theologians who I find especially helpful for understanding these themes are Leonardo Boff, Gustavo Gutiérrez, Letty Russell, and Jung Young Lee.

For Boff, the church is where the Spirit is, regardless of established clerical structures. His 1977 book *Ecclesiogenesis* defended base ecclesial communities to the Catholic authorities, arguing that these communities celebrate the marks of the church and are spaces for living out life in Jesus Christ. His theology and understanding of the church's mission is based on Matthew 25; his analysis of this passage identifies the only difference between nonbelievers who feed the hungry and clothe the poor and believers who do so. The disciple is surprised when Jesus says that all of these good deeds had been done to him. For Boff, we (believers/the church) know what we ought to do, and will not be surprised. We inherently know what we ought to look like to be church.[42]

Gutiérrez complements this view with his understanding of the church as a journeying people of God.[43] Although he believes that the kingdom of God is already here through the action of the church and its history, "journey" is a key aspect of understanding the church. It is a continuous becoming, because the world is continuously changing. Letty Russell uses the ecclesiological image of the table. Her goal is to argue for the marginality of the church and its responsibility toward inclusion if it is to foster the kingdom of God. She brings a tangible and relatable understanding of church that is theological and sacramental at the same time. Here the church reaches out toward the kingdom of God by becoming a round table practicing inclusion, community, and feast.[44]

Finally, Jung Young Lee claims that if the essence of the church is Jesus, the church is the community of God's marginal people.[45] He argues that the Word was incarnate in marginality; as Jesus was marginal, so the church ought to be marginal. This does not mean perpetual suffering; rather, not standing at the margins means not having the full presence of God. The ills of today's church are its centralization, its imitation of empire. Liberation from the margins is the opposite of domination from the center. A church that works for the reign of God on earth cannot look like the empire, because the empire is of this world, but the kingdom of God is not of this world.[46]

These four theologians offer ecclesiological resources for the three themes I explore in analyzing Puerto Rican congregations as I argue that the church of Christ *is* what it *does*: social change, revolution, and liberation. For Boff, "community must be understood as a spirit to be created, as an inspiration to bend one's constant efforts to overcome barriers between persons and to generate a relationship of solidarity and reciprocity."[47] In other words, since the church is a visible community, it *is* what it *does*.[48] "Liberation" is the process of achieving freedom from oppressive and unjust practices that restrict human and nature's flourishing. "Social change" might certainly denote any change in society, positive or negative; however, for the purposes of this book it has the connotation of being change in the direction of liberation. Finally, "revolution" is a turnaround infused by a process of conversion that reaches out and marches toward human and creation's flourishing.

The work these theologians are proposing requires an immense amount of effort and commitment. In Lee, the contemporary ecclesial value of comfort is shaped by capitalism and not by the values of the kingdom.[49] The criteria for discerning ecclesiological practices that speak to these themes of revolution, social change, and liberation answers the question: Do these practices challenge the imitation of empire and capitalism as they face the evils of this world? In the remainder of this section I look at communion as a resource for social change, marginality as a resource for revolution, and Holy Spirit as a resource for liberation. These themes, interacting in the churches I analyzed, can articulate hope as well as foster it.

As a resource for social change: communion. Lived communion moves us towards social change as it inverts social order. It is a practice of inclusion and remembrance. According to Roberto Goizueta, the body of Christ is in a "communion ecclesiology," which therefore turns into a "borderlands ecclesiology." For Goizueta communion is *pueblo, familia, el pueblo crucificado*: the sacrament of God's reign.[50] The push for social change comes from the needs of the margins. Communion is a celebration and a sacrifice from the margins, for the margins, and because of the margins. Goizueta asserts that communion calls us to remember. Though remembrance is a theme further explored in the next chapter as a means of expanding on decolonial analysis, the practice of remembrance, in general, and remembering Jesus, in particular, helps us call into the present that which is not there and those who are missing from the table. Being at the table is not a matter of having a place at the center, but of partaking in the process of being community, fed and embraced in our full humanity. Furthermore, when Jesus calls us to remembrance it is not to remember his last supper, but to remember his life. In remembering his life, we remember his teachings; and in remembering his teachings, we remember his commands toward living out the kingdom of God.

Communion also has a component of preparation: preparation of the table and preparation for coming to the table. When we think about communion, we usually picture the table already set. We rarely think about those who make the bread and wine, those who clean the space and set the table, but they are critical elements of communion. The practices of forgiveness, repentance, and coming together are also elements of communion. Communion does not start at the table. Thinking about communion and about these "small practices of a new divine reality" helps us to look at how they can foster and influence social change in the larger society.[51]

Letty Russell speaks of the authority of the principle of the table as the Gospel understanding of the household of God. This household is fueled by what she calls "the fencing of the table" to establish the right administration of the gifts of God by living justly with those who are marginalized from Church and society.[52] "Fencing" here is not establishing limits but seeing where the limits of the table are and asking who is not there. I understand social change in an ecclesial context as intrinsically bound to social justice because the work of the church is the mending of creation's brokenness and, I would add, the prevention of its further brokenness. Several of the churches participating in the book project have ministries surrounding the sharing of meals. One of the challenges María's aftermath posed was the lack of food and/or the lack of access to it. Local congregations remembered their communities as they mobilized to feed those in need. Referring to the last supper and the meals Jesus shared with his disciples and with people marginalized by society, Leonardo Boff says these meals "have a salvific-eschatological meaning: God offers salvation to all, invites the good and the evil without distinction into an intimacy with God."[53]

As a resource for revolution: marginality. In a neo-capitalistic and self-serving society, what is more revolutionary than a vow of poverty? Jon Fife, a Presbyterian pastor and leader of the Sanctuary movement in the 1980s, speaks of how the work he and his church did for Salvadorian refugees does not compare to what the refugees did for them: saved their souls.[54] There is a fine line between being with the poor and using the poor. Therefore, I will speak about the practice of poverty as an example of marginality, not to glorify it or to objectify it but to understand it as a means for revolution. Poverty gives us a different lens—I would say a sharper lens—on reality.

Jon Sobrino, using St. Ignatius's theology of compassion to understand ecclesial wealth and poverty, says that the church of Christ is a poor church; a compassionate church is a poor church. Society, and therefore the church, is filled with hidden idols, and poverty brings truth into the light. A rich church fails to become flesh because it does not know how to meet the need in the road.[55] Sobrino even says that a wealthy church is not a human church because compassion inevitably reaches one's heart and gut so you can feel the other's suffering.[56] Although I am careful about not commodifying another's pain and calling on anyone to personally identify with another's suffering, I understand Sobrino's bold claims against a rich church. Poverty places us at the margins and unveils the practices of empire that enable poverty and creation's suffering.

For Letty Russell, God's option for the poor is the reparation of creation with God. She argues that relationships built from restoration foster solidarity, not fear.[57] This mending of relationships positions us toward social action and therefore toward revolution: a turnaround, a conversion of the social order toward liberation. After Hurricane María, according to my project's collaborators, local churches were forced to reflect on their work and mission to mend their relationships with the poor in Puerto Rico. The situation of María sometimes affirmed and refocused the church's commitment to the people.

As a resource for liberation: The Holy Spirit. In Puerto Rico, mostly in the Pentecostal tradition, there is extensive preaching about the fear of a constricted Spirit and the need for discernment about the things that constrict the Spirit. "Constricting" also translates into suppression, restriction. I understand the Holy Spirit as God and not as a subordinate being. I cannot recall any belief that one can suppress Jesus or suppress the Father. Therefore, there is something to be said about the Holy Spirit in relationship to liberation. If we understand the Holy Spirit as God-with-us and our *consolador*, and if we can oppress the Spirit and constrict it, it means that the Holy Spirit moves. Elizabeth Conde Frazier places the Holy Spirit at the cornerstone of *Evangélica* ecclesiology, since within a patriarchal ecclesial system the call to ministry for women happens through the charisma of the Holy Spirit. In a tradition where women are biblically and historically subordinate to men and where women cannot have the same authority and participation as men, the only explanation for the defiance of those beliefs is the power of the Holy Spirit, which "calls creation into its fullness for healing and liberation."[58] The Holy Spirit breaks through our petrified and atrophied theologies and practices. One cannot ultimately contain the Holy Spirit; therefore, its ontological character is liberation. According to Boff, Gutiérrez, and Moltmann, Pentecost is the beginning of *ecclesia*.[59] We cannot understand the church and its mission if we do not understand ourselves through the doctrine of the Holy Spirit, which fosters new life and maintains the church in history.

All these resources for the church—communion, marginality, the Holy Spirit— embody community. For Gutiérrez, the church must be a sign of liberation and celebrate its eschatological hope in social revolution.[60] These practices of sharing communion, living marginality, and welcoming the Holy Spirit open our imaginations and foster living out our hope of being the church for the world. The Holy Spirit frees us, marginality teaches us how to make *de tripas corazones* (hearts out of guts), and communion is a movement toward inclusion and diversification.[61] The final section of this chapter shows how participating congregations who are doing just that.

WEAVING FINDINGS

Hope

In this section, I describe my collaborators' definitions of hope—and where they place their hope. Unanimously, they described one of María's lessons as the realization that worldly systems were fundamentally hopeless. As collaborator #18 put it, *"lo material no es nuestra esperanza ni nuestra seguridad. Todo calló."*[62] Collaborators talked about not placing hope in material things.

Rather they spoke about hope in Jesus and the hope of living into his teachings. This same collaborator who spoke about everything failing was concerned that Puerto Rico not become a *pueblo* that does not know what hope is or what it hopes for because it believes only in what it can be certain of.[63] The collaborator mentioned how people's hope turns into a manipulation of their faith to achieve the desired outcome. María, for them, was a passing of God through the island, and they correlated the anguish of María to the anguish of the passion of Christ: *"La tribulación es parte de saber lo que esperamos."*[64] The material conditions do not change *the* hope. This collaborator, as well as several others, claimed that *"La esperanza nos tiene que mantener alegres."*[65] All my collaborators shared a tone of sadness when speaking about Puerto Rico, but when they mentioned their hope in Jesus, their demeanor and the energy in their voices changed.

According to my collaborators, hope is:

- *Jesús*.
- Being with Jesus, when being with those in need.[66]
- Trust that at the end of the day, things can be different and better.[67]
- Good humor and joy.[68]
- *"La esperanza trasciende lo que tenemos, la esperanza trasciende a lo que vemos. Es ese gancho al cual nos agarramos para poder cruzar el río de la dificultad. Sin esperanza nos morimos. Yo creo que la esperanza es lo que nos hace desear la vida, lo que nos hace desear un mañana, lo que nos hace movernos en direcciones opuestas a lo que sería nuestro querer."*[69]
- *"La esperanza nos puede llevar a nosotros a ser más sensibles y amar más junto con la fe. Es como un sueño. Está centrada en Cristo."*[70]
- Letting go of fear, trusting that God is accompanying us.[71]
- Something you share.[72]
- Seeing how God sees.[73]
- To live the experience of Jesus. It is not a perfect reality, but in it we find life to continue moving forward.[74]
- We, the people, are the hope enacted.[75]
- *"Que estas situaciones de tribulación nos ayuden a contemplar a Dios desde otra realidad."*[76]
- *"La esperanza está en el que nosotros estamos siendo capacitados."*[77]
- "Hope is the idea that there are these unseen realities that are more real than the seen realities, and that one day its fullest embodiment will happen."[78]
- *"Esperanza es la virtud de esperar que las promesas de Dios por el bienestar de su pueblo serán cumplidas siempre."*[79]

These definitions resonate with the ways hope has been articulated in the previous chapters. Understanding hope as keeping us joyful resonates with the attitude of *a mal tiempo, buena cara* discussed in chapter 2. Hope is seen as a form of transcendence toward an unseen future that manifests itself in the present through the ways we hold on to and practice being and sharing the good news to others. It predicates, as Anzaldúa proposes, a different reality. Hope is more than a passive expectation. We trust that in the wait, and in people's disposition to serve others, the Holy Spirit is working and "training" people for the work to come. Hope is full of contradictions and shaped by people's material conditions. Nonetheless, within the Christian tradition the life of Jesus and the Divine affirm the principle of hope as a hope that is practiced in everyday life.

Telos

The aims of my collaborators' hope can be summarized as "freedom," "justice," and "evangelization." In this section I analyze their responses about how they practice hope toward these ends under four organizing directives: be a prophetic voice, be coherent, have a plan, and be the hope.

Be a prophetic voice: All nineteen collaborators discussed the relationship of church and state and their understanding of the church's role in the political and public sphere, as prompted in the questions. Collaborators #12 and #13 conceptualized this relationship through their understanding of citizenship. Their political and public participation as representatives of the church's values, they believe, equates to and should be as valid as their rights of national citizenship. The latter is because, as individuals, they are embodying the church's values. Though an interesting angle, it leaves some room to question their understanding of church members who are not citizens.

Many collaborators had a more collective approach and argued the church should be a *voz profética* (prophetic voice) in relationship to the state.[80] They mentioned the thin line the church has walked many times, having a hard time distinguishing its role in politics. Collaborator #4 critiqued the Puerto Rican church, mainly the Protestant church, arguing that it is mostly known for what it opposes rather than for what it proposes. Their congregation's community organizing project, by contrast, is trying to create a public image for the church as a proponent rather than an opponent of state practices. Others alluded to systematized evil or the evil within society's systems. They argued that in order to bring justice the church's prophetic voice should not focus on individuals, but on the systems that perpetrate evil.[81] (In chapter 4, I will problematize the practice of being a prophetic voice through the lens of postcolonial theory and the subaltern as a form of unveiling the complexities of the church being called to prophesy in a colonized context.)

Be coherent: I asked my collaborators about the public sphere's distrust of the Christian church in Puerto Rico due to a perceived lack of integrity. Collaborator #1 spoke about the church's and individual believers' actions as lacking coherence: "*Ahí es que en la experiencia que uno va teniendo con la gente uno es una causa de bendición y una alternativa creíble del poder de Dios.*"[82] Collaborator #4 said: "*La esperanza, antes de ser comunitaria tiene que nacer dentro de ti, vivo mi esperanza con mi ejemplo. La esperanza no se puede fingir por mucho tiempo, la esperanza nace dentro de ti entonces se desborda.*"[83] Two collaborators mentioned that regaining trust in *el pueblo* requires listening and being in solidarity.[84] This solidarity needs to be a *solidaridad viva* (live solidarity).[85]

Have a plan: Collaborator #4 spoke about an *esperanza práctica* (practical hope) as one that builds visible projects that works *with* the community so they can see what was once destroyed they themselves were able to build up again. This collaborator saw hope as intertwined with change.[86] In my research, ministers and lay leaders recognized the importance of working with the religious and the social imaginary in dialogue. Several collaborators alluded to this lack of dialogue, and three of them prescribed a *proyecto de pueblo* or *proyecto de país*, a national project, as a necessary solution.[87]

This phrase requires some unpacking. In Puerto Rico, and especially within the Protestant tradition, speaking about political and patriotic activism can be seen as anti–United States and bordering on communism. Although for some of us this might not be a big deal, the church in Puerto Rico carries—or better said, drags—a heavy discourse and practice around US assimilation. Because of this history, to be liberative and inclusive and not fall into gatekeeping tendencies, a *proyecto de país* drafted by the church needs to participate with the already established efforts of community organizations to move the country forward. These might include *Casa Pueblo, El Departamento de la Comida,* and *Juntegente,* initiatives on renewable energy, agriculture, and economic development respectively.[88]

A *proyecto de país* works toward the definition of political status.[89] "*Jesús vino a descolonizar.*"[90] A *proyecto de país* participates and collaborates for the purpose of the greater good, rather than for more laity in the pews.[91] A *proyecto de país* takes into account the material conditions that reinforce Puerto Rico's oppression.[92] A *proyecto de país* includes the Puerto Rican diaspora, who, as María passed, poured themselves out in their desperation to care for the island and its inhabitants, shattering the prejudice and elitism around the question of who gets to be "Puerto Rican." What worked during that time, and is working, is communitarian service, the bonds of unity and the call for justice.

Be the hope: "*La mejor teología es la que se vive.*"[93] When I asked my collaborators, "How do you live out your hope?" they mostly answered, "I am the hope." The people I spoke with believed in a chain reaction of sharing hope and motivating others to participate in this hope by being at the service of others and accompanying them through their experiences.[94] Embodying Jesus's teachings, as a Christian responsibility, brings people to believe they can be the hope society needs. People spoke about this embodiment as individuals and as the church interchangeably, meaning that when they spoke about their roles as Christians they spoke about the role of the church at the same time. To most of them the church was the people, the assembled community.[95] Regardless of its erring humanity, the church is a symbol of hope.[96] When speaking about the aftermath of María, they said, *"La iglesia definitivamente fue una de esas arterias por donde la sangre de la esperanza circuló para llegar a familias."*[97]

CONCLUSION

A buen entendedor, pocas palabras bastan: for those who understand, very few words are needed. In this chapter, although in many words, I showcase the living-out of people's hopes, how they are church through their actions. Since none of my collaborators emphasize a religious *discourse* of hope, coming up with a definition was the most difficult part of the interview for many of them. However, talking about their hope and how they embody it, and how they see the church as embodying it, came easily. They understood the possibility of change through their actions, and through their trust in God they could believe in the transformation of society. The interviews in this half of the chapter complement the section on ecclesiology and social movements, as they affirm the theory with a presentation of its working on the ground. These congregations' outreach programs focused on work with the most vulnerable (marginality) in their communities through the sharing of resources (communion) as a call from the Divine (Holy Spirit). In the upcoming chapters, I will continue to draw from the collaborators' proposal for a *proyecto de país* as a potential locus for an ecclesial transformative and liberative movement that enacts sustainable hope in public.

Chapter Four

About the Future: *"Vivir del Cuento"*

The expression *vivir del cuento* can be translated in several ways. *Vivir del* means "to live out of" or "to live into." *Cuento* translates to "tall-tales" or "fantasies," if one wants to use its negative connotation. For a more positive version, *cuento* can translate to mean "stories" and "narratives." If it's stretched a little, it can also mean "dream." In popular culture, the expression is often used pejoratively, meaning that someone is naïvely living into their fantasies. In this chapter, however, I will focus on the relationship of hope and memory. *Cuentos* get passed on, traditioned, as cultural capital or in more intimate spaces like family circles. Memories are not only shaped by events but by narratives, *cuentos*. Through *cuentos*, memories can inform the ways we live into our hopes; they can be either illusions (false memories) or sustainable hopes (memories that ground us in our realities).

Drawing on the field of memory studies, specifically research on collective memory, I explore the existing imagination and imaginary of Puerto Rican society: from knowing where one is to envisioning where one can go. Scholarly literature often regards memory as an unreliable aspect of the human condition.[1] But for others, including Walter Fluker, Gustavo Gutiérrez, and Joseph R. Winters, remembering, or bringing to memory, holds the key to resistance as it paves the path to liberation in *la lucha*.[2] In claiming memory as a key aspect of hope's sustainability, I will engage liberation theology, decolonial and postcolonial studies, and political theology to envision a practice or practices of hope that promote a change from "living out of the tall-tale" to "living into the dream" (our imagination). These frameworks provide a scaffolding of hope that looks into a future that can draft a *projecto de país* (national project) as articulated by my project collaborators.

MEMORY

One of the most interesting characteristics of memory is its capacity for elasticity. Memory is rarely, if ever, static; it can be retained, constructed, reconstructed, re-membered, and erased. Memory can also overlap with imagination: for example, in dreams, where imagination and memories of our realities come together. Walter Benjamin speaks about how we live our lives through information and storytelling, emphasizing how the information we have limits our imagination.[3] When this dichotomy of information and imagination fuses into one, we cannot see how we are living from *el cuento*. We engage reality with fiction; we live out of tales we embody as real. Fictional narratives (tall tales) are embedded in social memory and behavior as part of the construction of our society. Memory can be selective and indistinguishable from reality. "The struggle of man against power is the struggle of memory against forgetting."[4]

I am curious about the construction and power of memory. But what happens when our imagination-memories move into the real world? When I was around six years old, learning how to read, my uncles gave me a customized book for Christmas. It told a story about me going with Santa Claus to deliver presents to all my family and friends. I knew fairy tales were not real, but this book had my name and all of my friends' names in it. I was sad because I could not remember this ever happening. Plus, the kid in the story had straight hair, unlike me. So, I asked my mom if this had really happened, and she confirmed it. I was not raised to believe in Santa Claus because it was a US tradition, so you can imagine my confusion. Nonetheless, I had my mother's testimony and the text as proof. I not only started to believe that the story was true, I started to recall it as a memory.

Memory, whether "real," imagined, or some hybrid of the two, provides a cognitive map. It creates a chain of tradition between past and present and fills in the gaps in order to give society continuity.[5] Since this is so, for the purpose of articulating a hope instead of an illusion, I am interested in understanding how memory works within colonialism—namely, how agency is restricted and political patterns are forged as communal and individual memories. I am also interested in seeing how remembering and the retrieval of "lost" memories can be part of an awakening and disrupting of colonialism and neocolonialism. Memory impacts hope to the extent that it impacts society's conception of a future.

For psychoanalyst Doris Laub, memory takes root in the concrete, and witnessing to memory can break collective delusion as it is tied to collective discourse. Although Laub's research specifically focused on victims of the Holocaust, her work can speak to the reality of the "unwitnessed" trauma of

Puerto Ricans' colonial history as individuals and as a society. In this context there is a collective "delusion" in rituals, stories, and memory, where reality and trauma are "disjointed" and where to a great degree society is living from *el cuento*.[6] What would the role of the witness be? How do we heal memory in the face of a constructed reality? Memory engages with many levels of power relationships.[7] For Maurice Halbwachs, "the mind reconstructs its memories under the pressure of society."[8] It is influenced by what Chris Weedon and Glenn Jordan call state gatekeepers: our institutions that facilitate the process of remembering and forgetting.[9]

In the process of colonizing bodies, epistemologies are also formed. Memories are shaped in order to sustain a set of unifying practices that join societies through developing an identity or citizenship. Scholars such as Maurice Halbswachs, Paul Connerton, and Pierre Nora see religious rituals as important to the construction and continuity of collective memory. Rituals are therefore also important to the process of decolonization. Religious rituals do not only connect us to a past that we enact in the present, but project into the future, which for Christianity means a future hope. True liberation ought to be holistic, healing the body, the spirit, and the memory of both individuals and of society. Forging a *proyecto de país* as the means for a sustainable hope requires deep analysis of the material and epistemological effects of, and conditions of oppression through, colonization. Puerto Rico's memory and history, fragmented and corrupted, struggles to find liberation through Puerto Rican society's collective memory.

Collective Memory and its Characteristics

Before returning to the question of how collective memory surfaces in Puerto Rico, in this section I introduce three scholars of collective memory who not only have significantly shaped the field, but who focus much of their work on how societies remember through rituals, as well as the influence of religion in memory: Maurice Halbwachs, Paul Connerton, and Pierre Nora.[10]

The work of Halbwachs, a French philosopher generally understood as the pioneer of collective memory studies, was greatly influenced by his teacher and mentor Émile Durkheim. From a sociological standpoint, memories, concepts, souvenirs, and the information we retain foster our actions toward others and informs our engagement within the collective. One of Halbwachs's most important contributions is the distinction and correlation between the individual and the collective, and the autobiographical and the historical. Although collective memory is that which is kept in the collective, individuals are the people doing the remembering. Historical facts are remembered differently by each individual in the collective, thus accounting for memory's fluidity. For Halbwachs, memory depends on the social environment.[11]

Halbwachs identifies and classifies collective memory in three groups: family memory, religious memory, and class memory. Family memories are those memories negotiated in the domestic sphere. However, they regulate our relationship with society. Collective memory is always in relationship to society, regardless of how many people are retaining the memory. For Halbwachs, every society is regulated and/or influenced by religion, so religious memory reconstructs and gives continuity to collective memory. Finally, class memory fosters the traditions within class divisions, showing that operations in society are mediated (structured) by collective memory.

Collective memory shows how minds work together as it extends as far as the group composing it.[12] Memory is a matter of construction, which is why sometimes we wake up and ask ourselves, "Did I dream that or did it happen?" It is also why I can remember going on Santa's sleigh. More importantly, it is why political manipulation through memory can be socially detrimental. Halbwachs writes, "Memory . . . is first of all a matter of how *minds work together* in society, how their operations are not simply *mediated by social arrangements* but are in fact *structured* by them."[13] The emphasized phrases set up the scaffolding of the power of memory but also display the active and mechanical aspect of it. Social arrangements do not simply mediate or interpret our collective activity, including the activity of producing collective memory; they structure this activity.

French historian Pierre Nora is famous for his analysis of *lieux de mémoire* (places of memory), places that crystalize and secrete memory. Nora divides Western history of memory into three time periods: Pre-Classical, Classical, and Modern. In the Pre-Classical stage, "natural memory" was fostered by environments of memory and sustained by place-based rituals and traditions which made memory part of everyday life.[14] The Classical stage was marked by the nineteenth- century era of industrialization, as collective memory passed into the hands of the elite who began producing "sites of memory."[15] And in the Modern era, the ideology of nation-state collapses, and memory becomes society's knowledge of itself; history is a field of social science and memory is part of the private sphere.[16]

Tracing this history, Nora establishes the notion of *lieux de mémoire* (places of memory) because there is no *milieu de mémoire* (center of memory).[17] Places like plazas, monuments, and palace secrete memory. Places of memory have to be material, symbolic, and functional; otherwise, they are just historical. The *Museo de la Revolución* in Havana, Cuba, for example, secretes memory in Nora's sense. It is housed in the former presidential palace and its new use, not to mention the bullet holes it still retains from the revolutionaries' final assault, serves as a constant symbolic and material reminder of the past. Another example, closer to my interests, is the Christian church. Take the United Methodist Church in Spanish Harlem, New York, a place marked by the struggles of the community and the beginnings of the Young Lords.[18] For Nora, society renounced memory as it banished ritual, and what we have now is a second order of memory as we observe *from* and not *the* substance of memory.[19] Regardless of where memory comes from in society, the collective will search for coherence in society and its cohabitation. There is a risk, however, of inventing tradition arbitrarily as society searches and articulates its memory.[20]

British social anthropologist Paul Connerton's seminal work *How Societies Remember* speaks of memory as not always being in the cognitive sphere. Memory is also a tangible experience in society through commemorative ceremonies and bodily practices.[21] Influenced, like Halbwachs, by Durkheim's claim that societies need to revive and reproduce their accomplishments as a group, Connerton identifies rituals and ceremonies as the way society remembers. Re-enactments and the commemoration of continuity shape communal memory, with images and knowledge of the past sustained by performance.[22]

Collective memory, according to these and other theorists, shapes and builds our sense of identity. The Christian church shapes Christian identity, but as we know through history and experience, it also shapes national identity in many places and among many peoples. More and more through the years, Puerto Rican political discourse has been filling in the gaps of historical fragmentations as it tries to make peace with its perennial colonial status. At the extremes of the plurality of identities (including political)[23] in Puerto Rico, one can find two quite distinct stereotypes of an assimilating right and a liberationist left. The in-between is undecided, but we all grapple within a wide range of *cuentos*. In a lot of ways Puerto Rican memory is a *cuento*.[24]

The notion of collective memory, as elaborated by these three theorists, helps us to understand the scaffolding of how Puerto Ricans function as a group as well as the reservations of a good majority of the population in relationship to the Christian church, particularly its presence in the public sphere. This tie of collective memory to ritual opens up a venue (which I will explore further using postcolonial theology) that presents a fourth political alternative—neither right, left, nor center—for agency in the construction of decolonial practices and the shaping of the image of the Christian church in Puerto Rico through practices of hope. The goal is not just a remembrance of history, but an owning of it.

Memory studies help identify the continuity and the shifting of social frames. It is not always easy to identify all the levels of how collective memory surfaces in national and religious discourse, culture, politics, places, and events. And it is also instructive to realize that constructed collective memories can become acceptable and unacceptable as the social frame enabling them shifts. I am all grown up, so to say that I still remember my adventures with Santa is not as cute as when I was six years old. It is a social consensus that the story of Santa Claus is a *cuento*, a fairytale, not acceptable for adults to believe. It *is*, however, acceptable for me to think of Jesus as white, because this is the way he has been remembered in colonial popular culture and religious discourse. But it is controversial to depict him in his historical Middle Eastern context and skin tone. Political shaping makes it acceptable for me to sing the Puerto Rican national anthem that embodies the "beauty" of Puerto Rico's colonial captivity, but seditious and offensive to sing the Puerto Rican revolutionary anthem, which preceded the current one.[25] In understanding how minds work together (collective memory) we can see the continuity not only of the commemoration of the past, but how the past and its commemoration shapes our present! Seeing the thread will hopefully lead us into shaping another future full of possibilities and hopes, with fewer *cuentos* in the pejorative sense.

FORGETTING AND REMEMBERING

The shaping of collective memory plays between forgetting and remembering. Both practices have a significant impact on memory, in positive and negative ways depending on the context. There are instances when the acts of remembering and forgetting are arbitrary to the neurological functions of the individual. However, collective remembering and forgetting require intentionality. For Halbwachs, remembering "provides individuals and collectives with a cognitive map, helping orient who they are, why they are here and where they are going. Memory, in other words, is central to individual and collective identity."[26] Collective memory is, therefore, vital in order to form/belong to a group. Collective memory offers an order to the past, and the creation of master commemorative narratives structures this memory by giving a storyline.[27] Additionally, "The master commemorative narrative focuses on the group's distinct social identity and highlights its historical development [. . .] the group reconstructs its own history from a current ideological stance."[28]

In order for a group to develop such an enclosed and hermetic narrative, it needs also to forget, therefore, to suffer from "collective amnesia;" remembering and forgetting go hand in hand.[29] Some of the dangers of these types of practices in remembering and forgetting are the manipulation of history and the promotion of political agendas, for this narrative tends to represent the political elite's portrayal of the past.[30] This tension between remembering and forgetting also questions the ethics of memory and the sense of commitment and mutual respect for a group/individual. Paul Connerton writes that memory as a social habit requires the exercise of cognitive memory's application of rules and codes, "or from the failure to apply them, we infer that a particular rule or code has been remembered or forgotten."[31] If collective memory depends on rules, then, in the face of colonization and the desire for the retention of power, one must ask who or what is orchestrating the *cuentos* and for what purpose the *cuento* unifies the people.

Mexican psychologist Jorge Mendoza García argues that forgetting was a legislated practice in ancient Greece, with people legally instructed to forget, for example, defeat in war. Mendoza García claims that institutions work to erase memory because progress based on power has no memory.[32] Forgetfulness is forged initially with silence, distance, and absences. What is not told comes to seem as if it did not happen and is erased from collective memory, or at least comes to lack meaning.[33] This forgetting generates holes in a culture's memory and takes away its richness.[34] Mendoza García draws his specific examples about the workings of willful institutionalized memory erasure from Mexico's period of dictatorship. In these decades those in power tried to minimize the collective effects of its terror by silencing. When they could not silence, they changed the language of their tactics and developed preemptive strategies to mitigate any upsurge for the purpose of substituting memory.[35] This does not mean that the hole is empty; it is filled with that which is lacking. It is a reminder that something was there.

In his book *Public Forgetting: The Rhetoric and Politics of Beginning Again*, Bradford Vivian calls to our attention studies on the memory of non-Western nomadic groups to delineate other frameworks of remembering and forgetting.[36] He emphasizes the important cycle of remembering and forgetting, vouching for the importance and value of forgetting because it gives room for something new:

> For some, memory is the dawn that banishes the darkness of night, the darkness in which our works and days recede into oblivion. But the evening of forgetting need not signify a terminal end to memory. Memory needs the freedom of its evening, the repose that tempers its heart and light. Those things that shimmer in the radiance of morning can endure among the shadows of evening, even in dramatically eclipsed form, waiting to be anew when morning breaks again.[37]

Although I agree this is one possibility, Vivian's concept remains limited to seeing memory as an uninterrupted cycle and serves as a privileged point of view of a memory. Ada María Isasi-Díaz provides a wonderful metaphor that speaks to this. She refers to culture as a garden, recognizing the natural changes and cycles that a garden goes through. Isasi-Díaz uses this metaphor to establish how problematic and harmful the violent imposition of cultural oppression on minority groups is, saying, "Forced changes bring not flourishing but wilting and dying."[38] Halbwachs warns against the cult of the past, mythologizing and mystifying it to the point of adding to it attributes that in reality it did not possess. But what I speak about is giving the cycle of memory the time it needs to shape and transform without violence.[39] Isasi-Díaz is not speaking directly to memory; however, it is not difficult to see the parallels and interconnectedness in this metaphor by understanding that culture is also shaped by memory, just as memory forms identity, which is passed on from generation to generation through culture.

Forgetting, for Vivian, allows space for society to be creative in forging new memories and new narratives that keep societies moving forward. However, letting go of practices sustained by oppressive and manipulated memories does not require us to forget. Communities that have been marginalized and oppressed are able to move forward by being able to recount their stories, tradition their memories, and *luchado* (struggle/fight) to live into their future daily. Memory can resist colonization. For ethicist Teresa Delgado, Puerto Rico's colonial history has forced amnesia on the collective consciousness.[40] Living into memories shaped by the imposition of a colonial narrative sets the collective up to dwell in and tradition false memories, illusions, tall tales. When new stories continue to be forced into the tall tales of the colonizer, it is only a matter of time for people to realize the lie and it becomes an epistemological *lucha*.

EPISTEMOLOGICAL *LUCHA*

In Latinx theologies, the phrase *lo cotidiano* ("the quotidian" or everyday) signifies the articulation of common visible practices in the Latinx community. *Lo cotidiano* touches not only physical practices but epistemological constructions, expanding *la lucha* into the imaginary and the ways of knowing that impact ways of being. Although people/society might have forgotten why they engage in certain practices that seem "natural," and although people might seem to act before thinking, there is a cognitive and epistemological principle behind it at all times. There's a *facultad* that moves one into action, whether people can articulate it or not.

To explain how this works in societies, I use the analogy of the set-up file for software programs. Once you install the software, you typically delete the installation file. The program works, but we forget how it got there in the first place and the codes that created and established it. The program does not work out of will but out of its set-up instructions. At the risk of being minimalistic, our actions are prompted by what we retain in our memory, both conscious and unconscious, both individual and collective. Part of the epistemological *lucha* of the colonized mind is to come to realize the operation and source of these constructions, realizing that actions and practices are bound both to the stories *told* and the stories *erased* from the collective as a form of control and oppression. This is part of the colonized society's *cotidiano*. I do not look to privilege knowledge over body, but rather to show that these two cannot be separated. We can speak about them in dichotomous ways and segregate them as we speak of them individually, but in practice, in the tangible world of *lo cotidiano,* body and mind work together.

Memory is not only a piecemeal recollection of past events; it is the narrative in which remembered events are embedded. Control of which narratives are told and which are forgotten is one of the key battles of colonial and decolonized memory. Literature scholar Arcadio Díaz Quiñones says of Puerto Rico:

> Como no es ni "latinoamericano" "ni norteamericano" termina por borrarse. Muchos no ven ahí ni sujeto histórico, ni fines. *La historia puertorriqueña es un relato que no cuenta, y que, por consiguiente, no se cuenta.* No está ni antes ni después, está fuera, sin complejidad, sin heterogeneidades internas, sin tensiones políticas y afectivas. Es el puro no ser. La exclusión ha sido la norma. *Lo puertorriqueño es una eterna frontera ignorada y despreciada, o un espacio neutro tratado con desconfianza.* Las categorías nacionales y culturales dominantes en los Estados Unidos y en Latinoamérica, y *la situación colonial puertorriqueña,* llevan con frecuencia a negar la memoria histórica, o a situarla en un "afuera" desdeñoso o paternalista, y casi siempre enigmático. *Es una memoria muchas veces negada, y rota.*[41]

Díaz Quiñones is mourning a broken memory due to the lack, and sometimes erasure, of Puerto Rican history, which eventually results in the creation of the subaltern.

Gloria Anzaldúa, in a similar vein, uses the analogy of *Coyolxauhqui* to speak of brokenness and fragmentation—not only cognitive fragmentation but the fragmentation of the body and the spirit. When I speak of epistemology, I am referring to ways of knowing and the ills of a colonial mindset, but this is not limited to cognitive knowing. It includes all of the ways people carry knowledge: through body, mind, and soul. *Coyolxauhqui* is the Aztec moon goddess. Her head was ripped off from her body and thrown into the heavens to form the moon, while her body was thrown in the abyss and lies there fragmented. Anzaldúa finds herself, especially her writing, in *Coyolxauhqui*'s fragmented state of body, soul, and mind. Coloniality of power (in Anibal Quijano's phrase) fragments, breaks, and sometimes erases, people's and creation's wholeness.[42] Anzaldúa argues that, "The *Coyolxauhqui* imperative is to heal and achieve integration. When fragmentations occur, you fall apart and feel as though you've been expelled from paradise."[43] Although it is hard to think and act positively in these times of *Coyolxauhqui,* "it is exactly these times of dislocation/separation that hold the promise of wholeness" and "bear witness to what our bodies remember."[44]

As this discussion suggests, our bodies are also places of memory.[45] Epistemological *lucha* through memory brings to the forefront the "dangerous memories" ethicist Walter Earl Fluker speaks about when addressing the faith of the African American community, a development from Johann Baptist Metz's term.[46] Dangerous memories are the forgotten, erased memories of other "worlds of meaning" that, along with the possibilities of redemption, move those who struggle into a place of hopeful faith and courage.[47] They are dangerous, specifically, to the present order of colonial power, which prefers and insists that certain things not be remembered. Before a hope is born out of an affirmation that "all will be right eventually," hope needs to be "translated through memory: a return to *the day before yesterday*, where the voices long lost and forgotten are given permission—better, opportunity—to join the conversation . . . They allow recovery of dismembered bodies of experience otherwise invisible to the consciousness."[48]

As I briefly mentioned in chapter 3, the use of mnemonic devices—sometimes hidden in cultural productions—ties communities to past events that help them move into action in the present. Sociologist Roberto Vélez, calling the struggle for Vieques to mind, argues that "the capacity of mnemonic practices to provide meaning to current events in light of the past, and potentially directing future ones, bring about the quality of memory to engage audiences into action" because of its "triggering power."[49] *Paz para Vieques* has been the greatest—in terms of scale—success of community organizing and political victory in contemporary Puerto Rican history. Mentioning or remembering it is the mnemonic device *par excellence* in Puerto Rican culture, showing the realization of hope through its pursuit and practice. It has now become a dangerous memory that (in Fluker's words) "involve simultaneous acts of weeping, confession, and resistance," opening a future that is, although still uncertain, hopeful.[50] Memory, through its articulation of a mnemonic model, transitions from cognitive liberation to embodied mobilization. The next section focuses on this transition.[51]

LIBERATION

Roberto Vélez is speaking of collective political mobilization in the work towards liberation. However, the path from conscience to action is not necessarily linear; *del dicho al hecho, hay un gran trecho*.[52] As mentioned in previous chapters, Rubem Alves's *Tomorrow's Child* proposes the need for a new beginning that rids society of oppressive organization. How do we do this? In

A Theology of Human Hope, Alves writes that hope "is committed to naming the things that are absent."[53] In *The Poet, The Warrior, The Prophet*, Alves speaks of the void of silence, the void of God. This void, as it relates to the void that was before creation, is a void of creativity, and hope fills the void with that which is absent. This void is identified by those who are oppressed, who are also the ones jumping into the void to bring about a new creation, or the materialization of what is lacking.[54] I see this "staring into the void" in the congregations that participated in my project, especially in the incorporation of lament in the congregation's services, and their looking towards what is missing in their mission and thinking about a future that is yet to come. For historical political reasons, the church in Puerto Rico has struggled to make the connection between the gospel and liberation. It was surprising to see collaborators speaking about colonialization since it is language typically deemed subversive and politically inclined, but there is no way to justify the colonial blinders anymore.

Gloria Anzaldúa invites scholars and writers to begin imagining a different world, grounded in spirituality, that is willed into creation and spreads out to begin healing the world.[55] In this work I propose an understating of liberation theology through acts of creation and imagination that are able to hold a complexity of angles, rather than a linear understanding, of the work towards freedom—a spiral in movement. Classic Latin American liberation theology and Black liberation theology mostly argue a liberation through history and point to the biblical story of Exodus. Expanding on classical texts of liberation theology, in this section I argue that a creation, rather than an exodus, model of liberation incorporates history, space, and bodies.[56] Liberation through history transcends the present and forms part of a process of struggle for better relationships with the world and all of creation. Nonetheless, this history is enacted and contextualized in space via bodies.[57] A creation hermeneutic enables us to hold and understand other ways of being and other ways of knowing. One has to be aware of how everything works together, given that creation incorporates a plethora of elements into a whole. Although Gustavo Gutiérrez focuses on Exodus, he also sees creation as a salvific act.[58] Through the process and continuous perpetration of colonization, history, spaces, and bodies have been apprehended and manipulated to benefit economic and capitalist interests, excluding those suffering from the vestiges of colonization while at the same time denying salvation from suffering. For decades, for example, not just since María, disaster capitalists have taken advantage of Puerto Rico's vulnerabilities and exploited them. A fuller theology of liberation needs to speak about the decolonization of time, space, and bodies. Practices of remembering for the sake of liberation accounts for a piecing-together of all of these elements, not only piecing together history by recounting events. Exodus is not liberation in a post-María Puerto Rico. Also, if history serves as a lens to foretell Puerto Rican liberation, 500+ years of colonization beg to differ from a perspective of progress in political liberation and autonomy, given that the situation has not progressed towards an amelioration of conditions.

A lens of creation that incorporates time, space, and bodies negates an escapist model to alleviate the suffering generating from the void. In Puerto Rico, creation happens in place. This creation reclaims what has been taken away from it and makes it anew. For some people, leaving in María's aftermath was their salvation. I recognize that sometimes it is necessary for people to flee to free themselves from oppression and death. Many people who depended on immediate medical assistance left the island in order to save their lives, for example, people who needed dialysis, or who were in the middle of cancer treatments, and so on. However, this exodus happens on an individual or much smaller scale of immediate family. Sometimes people simply wish to migrate, and why shouldn't they? A creation-rather-than-exodus approach in the context of a country like Puerto Rico expands from the individual as it tries to surround the whole. Exodus is not a matter of either/or, but it is problematic in a motive of liberation severing oneself from the collective memory that the land embodies.

In *Taíno* indigenous mythology, the human race was born out of a cave, *Cauta*, the magical mountain on the center of the island. This was the cosmic creation axis. There is a deep connection of creation to the ground and from the void.[59] Creation out of the void is more authentic to the development of a *proyecto de país* because it presupposes a renewal of the disintegration. The Cuban theologian Sergio Arce argues that creation is not something that is finished, but is a process.[60] He calls for a theology of reconstruction where "*Cualquier reconstrucción del pueblo significa fundamentalmente poner punto final a la 'fragmentación del ser humano.'*"[61] He points to creativity as the driving force of a Christian theology that responds to the call of the needs of society.[62]

History

Latin American liberation theologians like Gustavo Gutiérrez place the action of God's justice in history as the struggle for liberation in time as that which transcends present time, trusting the progression of liberation. However, memory, colonial forgetting, and the shaping of historical narrative (understood as part of the progress of history but not as the perpetration of evil in time) complicates the understanding of historical liberation.

For Rubem Alves, a colonized consciousness domesticates and deprives "its futuricity."[63] Alves relates this colonized consciousness to the adaptation and conformity of humankind to technology because the future is already realized in technology. He therefore complicates the progression of history through technology as a way of understanding liberation, saying, "The man who is the object of history, the being that fits in, that adapts to the given facts, is the man who loses his transcendence."[64]

Alves is not arguing against liberation through history, but rather exposing the complexities and limitations of history because of the systemic material constructions that entrap society and hinders its freedom from oppression. Alves unveils the illusion of historical transcendence—and perhaps exodus—and incorporates the concept of political humanism as one which is able to negate the present conditions and hope for something new. He proposes this concept in order to prescribe a *how-to* for the enactment of liberation.[65] This liberation happens in history, but at the same time it is directed by those who are able to envision freedom.

Space

Although technological advances allow for remote and innovative ways of colonizing today, commonly colonization began with the apprehension of the land. Puerto Rico, like other "underdeveloped" countries, has been exploited through the use and control of physical spaces for the purpose of industrialization, farming, and/or other types of developments that serve investors, making the land profitable for those who do not inhabit it and also displacing those native to it.[66] American Indian scholar George E. Tinker critiques liberation theology for its lack of acknowledgment of people's, especially indigenous people's, relationship to their land. He argues that for communities whose spirituality is rooted in creation, rationality and values are not only temporal but spatial.[67] He also warns that liberation theology's focus on an economic class, the poor, does not recognize the personhood of indigenous folks as it focuses on the capitalist categories of labor and means of production.[68] Tinker argues: "To put the means of production into the hands of the poor inevitably induces the poor to be exploiters of indigenous peoples and their natural resources."[69] American Indian spirituality asks *where* of the *basileia*, rather than *when*.[70] Again, exodus is problematic because it presupposes displacement without necessarily asking to whose benefit that displacement occurs.

Bodies

Mayra Rivera claims "Social arrangements meet us in the bodies of others."[71] Puerto Rican bodies have gone through forced sterilization, forced migration, work spoliation, the testing of Agent Orange, and the testing of the birth control pill, among other types of objectification of natives due to their assumed lesser humanity. As I mentioned in chapter 1, theologian Teresa Delgado analogizes Puerto Rico's colonial situation to that of a battered woman.[72] Oppression and violence happen to this body and it is therefore in need of liberation and healing. The imagery of the battered woman as a description of the relationship between Puerto Rico and its colonizers is too accurately disturbing. But some liberationist scholars have argued for the political agency of the vulnerable, refuting a paternalistic understanding that vulnerability is equivalent to passivity and weakness.[73]

Puerto Ricans and Puerto Rico's natural resources, especially its bodies of water, need liberation.[74] However, this need for liberation does not stem from a lack of strength, the need of a savior, or any other sort of paternalistic intervention. Instead, it is because Puerto Rican bodies, black and brown bodies in the United States, and their natural resources have been made sources of exploitation. Though not explicitly articulated as such, the non-white, the non-powerful, the subaltern's humanity is still in question: are they soulless? What if we shift to thinking about the most vulnerable bodies as the most valuable bodies?[75] Exodus presupposes "rescue" by the paternalistic savior. Maybe this epistemological change will change practices and move society to uplift the copious contributions of those whom coloniality erases.[76]

Political Liberation

For many liberation theologians (including M. Shawn Copeland, Gustavo Gutiérrez, and Leonardo Boff), liberation theology flows from and into political theories and practices. For Gutiérrez, liberation *is* political; thus, a church of liberation, as it reflects on its critical historical praxis gathered in ecclesia, needs to be part of the process through which the world is transformed.

All theology is political. Regardless of the church's public participation or its political influence in policymaking, the teachings of the church have political impact in the public sphere. A (self-identifying and self-aware) political church participates in the political arena. Listening to the cry of the oppressed, as Copeland says, demands that our theology be not just public but also political.[77] Liberation theology is also my hermeneutical methodology. Hence, I see political theology through the lens of liberation.

In her 2014 presidential address to the Catholic Theological Society of America, Copeland spoke of the three duties of a theologian: witness, memory, and lament. These duties also properly fit the church. For Copeland, witnessing is twofold, encompassing truth-telling and martyrdom.[78] Our English word "witness" translates as the Greek *martureo*, a legal term that meant to speak truly about an event or experience on behalf of someone else. "Witnessing," for Christianity, is never the act of a mere spectator but is a highly active and sometimes dangerous practice. Witnessing has consequences, but we must be willing to be discomfited and even to put our life on the line to witness a cry (protest) from the oppressed.

"Memory," for Copeland, means both protection and recovery.[79] She aims to acknowledge all stories and all groups. Political theology, at least for theologians like Copeland, resists homogenization. By having diverse voices at the table, we allow them to interrupt history as they offer us hope for amending our relationships. Infinite diversity also fights against the impulse of selective memory and makes us confront our "infected memories," thus giving us a glimpse of hope. Finally, for Copeland lament is both a prayer and a practice of justice.[80] Lament is not defeat. As a prayer, lament protests and pushes away the power of oppression. It also takes seriously God's compassion as it "boxes with God" and refuses to believe that our oppressed present is God's will. As a practice, lament announces publicly.

A witnessing church opens space for memory and lets testimony open up possibilities. Copeland is not proposing thought experiments or articulating a theorization of political theology; she is proposing a practical (practicing) political theology. In Puerto Rico (I would not say exclusively) the church has *poder de convocatoria* (power to summon). Sometimes that summoning is for causes that would seem contrary to the pursuit of social justice.[81] However, this *poder de convocatoria* can summon and spring hope in the collective, and I am personally hopeful seeing that after María, the Christian church is being more outspoken about the political status of Puerto Rico.[82]

The hope of political theology in the church is in its process of becoming a form that thrives for human flourishing. Theologian Dorothee Söelle uses Paul's "hope against hope" to refer to resistance; to hope is to resist.[83] Hoping, however, is tiring. It seems that we hope and constantly need to renew our hope. Politically, the church needs to hope against hope and find the inspiration and thrust to carry those who are tired of hoping. Cláudio Carvalhaes speaks about hope as strawberries you pick from the dirt. With the joy that comes with finding the strawberry, also comes the knowledge that the strawberry is ephemeral and will be consumed; however, you hope you can find another one along the way.[84] But then again, you cannot find them if no one has sown them. Political theology, according to Söelle, opens horizons, changes conditions, and fosters new life.[85] For Moltmann, "salvation which faith embraces in hope is therefore not a private but a public salvation, not only spiritual but also bodily, not a purely religious but also a political salvation."[86] Hope needs to be a public endeavor; hope needs to be political, of the people.

In an ecclesial context, a liberationist political theology that is accountable to community can be seen as restitution for all the times the church has been silent and for all the times its doctrine has crucified its own people. Political theology sets the theologian on a path of accountability and mutual responsibility. Political participation does not mean political power. Witnessing, lamenting, and remembering, as Copeland suggests, may actually gain the church many enemies. But as Gutiérrez beautifully reminds us, "it is those who try to 'save' the work of God who 'lose' it."[87] In other words, it is those who cling to ecclesial power in all selfishness who lose the work. To be a political church means to be a suffering and struggling church in living out hope. Within Christianity it takes the process Jesus began in his teachings to transform the world and gives continuity with the calling (summoning) of the kin-dom.

Puerto Rico's liberation of time, space, and materiality is bound to its political liberation, a far more complicated matter than choosing between independence and statehood. A hope, a dream, for liberation requires a decolonized understanding of hope that can hold and articulate the spaces that need to be free of colonialism to birth a creative proposal for a *proyecto de país*. Political liberation is equated to freedom; I say it is creative agency. Political liberation invites the creation of new alternatives that attend to Puerto Rico's flourishing.

THE POSTCOLONIAL SUBALTERN AND THE DECOLONIZATION OF HOPE

Not so long ago I posted a quote from Ramón Emeterio Betances,[88] a Puerto Rican freedom fighter, for the commemoration of *El Grito de Lares*, the 1868 revolt against the Spanish regime. I wrote: *"Nuestros enemigos no son tan grandes, es que nosostros estamos de rodillas."*[89] Five minutes later a friend replied, "It is on our knees that we win battles." We went back and forth on Jesus and his kneeling practices, and I argued that he was missing the point: Jesus never knelt to the Roman Empire. There are many "trigger words" that shut down political conversation both in the secular and ecclesial world, words like "socialism," "independence," and "material freedom." Churches in Puerto Rico often model the larger society's fears and anxieties around political issues. Most churches in Puerto Rico do their part in terms of humanitarian aid. However, it is not the norm to find a church that is denouncing systemic oppression. But this is a major problem, since colonization, even if it is not the root of all evil, is certainly an enactment of it. This section considers postcolonial studies' notion of the subaltern, an important reality when arguing about narratives and *cuentos*. Who gets to tell them?[90]

Postcolonial studies is a field that emerged from the academic work of the colonized and minoritized. Its analysis extends back to the early modern period of Spanish expansion—not because there were no pre-existing forms of colonization, but because at this time the Empire began practices of systemic othering through Casta rules. Postcolonial studies are complex, especially because there is really no "post" in colonialism, which in many places has simply shapeshifted to "neocolonialism." Nevertheless, to continue thinking and drafting a *proyecto de país* that can sustain hope for Puerto Rico and Puerto Ricans (whatever and whoever that means) requires using the lenses of subalternity and hybridity developed by postcolonial theory and exploring how subaltern and hybrid subjects are included in a process of liberation.

THE SUBALTERN

Theorist Gayatri Chakravorty Spivak is known for her work on "the subaltern," and is mostly referenced for her affirmation that the subaltern cannot speak. Postcolonial analysis always asks about power and hegemony. The subaltern is a person without social mobility, without the ability to escape a subordinate position in the hierarchy, and whom (Spivak argues) is also silenced.[91] Subalternity emerges in many aspects of life, including language. If I am writing in an academic context where English is the norm, *escribir en español revelaría una capa de mi ser subalterno que sólo deja de serlo porque mis lectores leen español.*[92] However, if my first language was Náhuatl or Quechua, that will be lost in the subaltern.

Enrique Dussel calls this reality "communication communities"; without a communication community there is no communication. His discussion of the subaltern defines them as the *inevitably* excluded. He categorically claims that there will always be affected people who will not be able to participate and will be excluded from "any real community of possible communication."[93] For Dussel, we live and operate within a presupposed world, and in this presupposed world there are three types of what he calls "affected": the excluded from discourse, the oppressed (exploited), and the materially excluded who cannot reproduce their life.[94] He voices the contradictions of this analysis by stating that "even though all the affected always have (an implicit) right to argumentative participation in the real community of communication, there is always some kind of exclusion to affect people."[95] There is always a tendency to leave someone outside. The important thing is to be aware of this and to understand the complexities of the dynamics of inclusion and exclusion as an ethical principle, seeing how "the Other represents the always possible beginning in disagreement (or origin of new discourse)."[96] For Dussel, this allows the continuous participation of the Other or the excluded-affected in the discourse. The involvement of the victims (the affected) interrupts history and creates new things.

Dussel discusses the ethics of liberation within this framework of the excluded and included in a community of communication and argues about the limits of this ethic in the face of revolutions, as they are considered "exceptional" situations in the face of asymmetrical processes of domination. He advocates for the inclusion of popular wisdom.[97] Dussel believes that popular wisdom will bring forward a communal and better-tuned approach in the emergence of the "ethical-critical conscientization" by the "affirmation of the value of the victims by the victims themselves."[98] With this approach, Dussel recognizes the value in the subaltern's (affected) agency and participation, something not well accounted for in postcolonial theory. He sees the subaltern (the affected) through the lenses of systemic oppression in the economic sphere.

Heavily influenced by liberation theology and transnationalism, Dussel is well aware of the dynamics of power, and what is at stake for him is life itself: the material aspects of life of all and for all. Theology in Puerto Rico, I argue, needs to be in constant dialogue with the public sphere for the sake of life and cohabitation in its relationship to power dynamics.

Pushing forward toward a "post" would mean making peace with our past and moving toward practices that do not continue to oppress and victimize peoples, for example, practices that do not reproduce systems of oppressive power and do not turn into a simple reverse of the hierarchy but create a model—perhaps, a legacy—that foments a cohesive praxis of justice. Doing this type of analysis in the Puerto Rican context, on and off the island, is a monumental task, but even more monumental is the task of putting it into practice. This analysis defies our ways of knowing, of being, and also believing. However, even as "hope" seems to rest on a future after migration from the island, I believe that wrestling with these proposals of a political and liberative theology in Puerto Rico moves people forward in reclaiming what is at stake in articulating a sustainable hope: a dignified life.

The question of the subaltern's identity and voice has continued to be central to postcolonial theory. Homi Bhabha, contrary to Spivak, says the subaltern speaks in the story of the subaltern, though I believe that talk about the subaltern does not mean the subaltern speaks.[99] Walter Mignolo speaks about subaltern rationality, which facilitates a border crossing within Dussel's communities of communication.[100] A liberation church witnesses to the subaltern (the oppressed) and understands how these layers of oppression work horizontally and feed off each other; it understands their intersectionalities. They are not just layers of hierarchy that we can peel off. In the case of Puerto Rico, this would mean noticing the migrants in our midst, recognizing other ways of being Puerto Rican in the diaspora, and letting the Puerto Rican diaspora speak. Also, as my interviews reflected, the church needs to keep its prophetic voice. It needs to be a church that denounces injustice and oppression of the marginalized. What would it mean to have a prophetic voice as the subaltern?

Nationalism, Diaspora, and Hybridity

Nationalism has had many meanings in the last two centuries, but within postcolonial critique it represents a place of resistance against imperial control in colonial societies. Analysis of nationalism, diaspora, and hybridity is also important in order to discuss who gets to speak and shape *cuentos*. The idea of "nation" is a shared community, an imagined community, which gives a sense of belonging and commitment to a group. For Frantz Fanon, a national culture validates itself as the people it created and its continued existence.[101] In the 1930s, Puerto Rican writers began articulating a national identity tied to the independence movement and the Catholic Church. Not all, but much, of how Puerto Ricans understand their identity comes from what these writers constructed. Puerto Ricans carry these notions of identity and nation through collective memory. Fanon, however, warns against the potential dangers of nationalism: hegemonic control, xenophobia, and the reproduction of patterns of oppression.[102]

In the United States, Puerto Ricans are the Latinx group most predominantly associated with the term diaspora.[103] Theologian Carmen Nanko-Fernández argues that "In Latin@ theological and Biblical studies, the image of diaspora, especially articulated by diasporic Puerto Ricans, reflects the ambiguities, tensions and multiple layers of complexities associated with possibilities of dislocation, bilocation, relocation and return available to colonized citizens."[104] With *diaspora*, the unity of national identity gets problematized. Diaspora is a combination of migration and continued cultural affiliation. Diaspora is understood as scattering and exile, always in relationship to cultural minorities. It fosters a sense of loss and even punishment, as its distance turns a people's sense of identity into a daily reconstruction which changes according to place and generation. For Edward Said, the diaspora can become a narcissistic masochism produced by isolation, displacement, and resistance to committing to the new place.[105] There is a pressure to join and belong and as well as a pressure to resist. Joining the new conditions in the foreign land causes the loss of critical perspective; not joining makes a fetish of exile by constantly resisting assimilation.

French philosopher Édouard Glissant coins the term *totalité-monde* to speak to the whole of the subject, to avoid the subject's compartmentalization, and to encourage the subject's relationships beyond a physical space.[106] Part of my task is to bring together the *totalité* (as much as possible, anyway) of Puerto Rico's history, memory, coloniality, beauty, expansion, and subjectivity (its people) in order to speak about hope. In *totalité* a liberatory *proyecto de país* for Puerto Rico must include the Puerto Rican diaspora. Even before the United Statesian invasion, there were Puerto Ricans living in exile in the United States. The relationship between islanders and Puerto Ricans in the diaspora is a sensitive topic.[107] The reception and welcome of the diaspora on the island varies from generation to generation depending on the migration wave. Diasporicans who have never been to the island or who do not speak Spanish—especially the second and third generations—are often considered less Puerto Rican by islanders, if seen as Puerto Rican at all. This matter of inclusion and exclusion is an important one, not only because it affects individuals in the assertion of their cultural identity and sense of belonging, but because it poses the question of who gets to decide in what direction a *proyecto de país* is drafted and who is included in that drafting.[108]

The problems with both "nationalism" and "diaspora" lead me to *hybridity* as an alternative to border consciousness, following Edward Said's recommendation to work through cross-border attachment rather than rejecting it. In postcolonial studies, hybridity is seen as a strength. Hybridity develops anti-monolithic models of cultural exchange and growth. Hybridity occurs at the imposition of assimilation and "conscious moments of cultural suppression" or with patterns of immigration.[109] Hybridity resists the idea of a pure culture but it is also how the oppressed culture survives (although one must also take into account cultural appropriation within hybridity).

The concepts of the subaltern, nationalism, and hybridity must be read together because together they mark the tensions and contradictions around political decision making, belonging, and theological groundings for Puerto Ricans. All three, however, require suspicion. There is no pure identity, and one must interrogate how much the dominant culture is imposing itself onto one's identity. For Albert Memmi, for example, there is no real assimilation, since the colonizer will never really accept the colonized as their own. The colonized can become the colonizer by seeing their reflection in the colonizer.[110] For those who are colonized persons in the colonized world, there is just no way of fully belonging; living on the island, living in the States, having one foot there and one foot here, one will always live in displacement, to some degree. It is worth noting, by the way, that for more and more new first-generation Christian Latinx immigrant communities in the United States, national identity is not as important as Christian identity. Pastor and theologian Ricardo Franco argues that in the life of the Latinx church, which is multicultural, congregants achieve better unity through their identity as Christians.[111] Without wanting to dismiss the deep connection people have to their Christian identity, I am concerned about the lack of attention to ethnic differences in collective spaces, as Christian identity can be embedded in colonialism and assimilation with US culture.

For many years, theology and the sacred were under-researched topics within postcolonial studies. It has only been in the last decade or two that the study of theology within a postcolonial framework (at least by title) has developed. However, it seems especially important to integrate the two areas; some postcolonial theorists have argued that theology is a key area of enfranchisement because more and more indigenous concepts of the sacred have interpolated the dominant culture.[112] The scant attention to theology within postcolonial studies is particularly surprising, then, since theology encompasses indigenous sacred concepts, providing a key space for local empowerment.

Within theology, on the other hand, attention to postcolonial theorists is significant, although recent. Theologian Vitor Westhelle, in his *After Heresy*, alludes to Schleiermacher's naïveté, referencing his affirmation on the impossibilities of heresies due to mission work and the Enlightenment, not seeing that this assumption is what gave way for indigenous faith to survive as a hybrid.[113] Westhelle argues that the true heresy is colonization, and that it is time for a retrieval of "heresies" as early expressions of postcoloniality.[114] Lewis Taylor, meanwhile, argues that Christianity is ignorant of its participation in neocolonialism, and postcolonial theology is only possible if it comes from a community of social practices that embodies the practice of postcoloniality.[115] He critiques postcolonial theorists for their inaccessible and abstract language. (Inaccessibility is not limited to postcolonial studies, but is a serious issue throughout all academic fields when the work of liberation becomes inaccessible for those who need to be liberated.) Taylor wants to uplift postcolonial theory's liberative power in the counter-imperial movement of Jesus and proposes four areas a postcolonial religious community should be aware of: the U.S.A. military and its colonial power; U.S.A.'s policy on Palestine; Islamic liberation movements; and penal system activism.[116] We must add to his list all the U.S.A. territories!

Postcolonial and decolonial approaches need not only articulate practices and methodologies for a liberative process, but also need to find approaches that include practitioners in conversation. It is urgent to fill in the gap between the deconstructive impulse of these fields and a creative *empuje* (push) and agency. Wonhee Anne Joh speaks about critical melancholia in relationship to postcolonial theology, claiming that it can be a dissatisfying field due to the constant blockage of a never-ending injustice.[117] Although I personally struggle with this melancholia, it is still true that the creativity that springs from hope comes out of collective work, out of border crossing, out of hybridity.

The struggle is beginning the conversation around these topics of religion, politics, and systems in order to face them. "*Yo soy yo y mis circunstancias . . .*" and postcolonial theology helps us know how theology of hope can move us forward without perpetrating coloniality.[118] For example, Puerto Rican missionary Jorge L. Bardeguez argues for a decolonizing liberation theology in Puerto Rico. For Bardeguez, a liberated church preaches a decolonizing Christ, struggles against the domestication of theology, separates itself from its founding imperial churches to create a Puerto Rican United Church, has a mission toward the poor and needy, and retrieves history to guide us forward.[119]

Although I largely agree with Bardeguez, I want to expand some of his points. First, as to preaching, there is a need to create a language that moves away from the academic discourse that is often forced onto people who already have developed impenetrable opinions about it. Instead, we should discern the spirit of what we desire and use language that is less fraught. For example, the term "socialism" is tainted by a century of propaganda against communism. Instead of preaching that we need to be socialist, we should preach on how our Christian practices are already engaging the underlying concepts behind socialism.

Second, as to Bardeguez's desired separation from founding churches, it is important to take into account people's senses of their affiliations and how their identities and beliefs are woven into those relationships. Forcefully removing or imposing a way of thinking can turn into another mechanism of oppression. Also, this approach implies that one can keep the tradition without its colonial inheritance. Third, partaking in a retrieval of history also includes unearthing the ways in which our ancestors also oppressed other people. The indigenous people of the island of Puerto Rico were "exterminated" and oppressed by Spain, but that does not mean they were exempted from oppression before colonization. Hence, retrieving history does not necessarily imply that we create a society that emulates our past; instead it shows us what not to repeat and move forward. There should be a caution sign in the task of historical retrieval. We spend so much time trying to collect the pieces of our past, and we do not spend enough time crafting a holistic and wholesome present and future.

Postcolonial and decolonial theories unveil the structures and practices of oppression and colonization, as well as other ways mechanisms of power result in social oppression. These theories continue to show us the objectification of beings deemed lesser than others and in need of control, as well as the impasses of our future as a society. Liberationist approaches that ignore these systems of oppressions and impasses that prevent the flourishing of society are themselves illusory. A postcolonial approach to hope helps us understand and deconstruct the cultural productions of colonialism. It lifts up an existential mirror to our practices and epistemologies and examines what we are made of. A decolonial approach provides a constructive lens. It includes other ways of being and knowing that help, even if just a little, to strip coloniality from ourselves. A decolonization of hope forces one to strip ourselves from illusions. Because we are constantly unveiling and reassessing our hope through its elasticity, a decolonized hope begins to shape a hope that is sustainable and accounts for those outside of our community of communication. Decolonial hope cannot mimic Empire.[120]

PRACTICES OF HOPE

What rituals of social change, liberation, and revolution can the church offer to help us move on into a postcolonial/decolonial future? Saint Paul Baptist church in New York celebrates a *Maafa* service each year, while a small congregation of Disciples of Christ in Puerto Rico worships with locally composed music and instruments typical of Puerto Rico.[121] What else might there be? I would not go as far as to say that the ways post-María churches in Puerto Rico are practicing their hope are fully decolonial, but they give a glimpse of what a real postcolonial future could look like. This is why turning to creation, more than to exodus, is so important to thinking about liberation. Sergio Arce Martínez focused his theological work around drafting what it would mean for the Cuban people, post-revolution, to understand their situation as one pregnant with the promise of creation.[122]

Hope steps into the void of the unknown in pursuit of creativity. This sounds poetic, but it is also practical. Take the nights Puerto Rico spent in complete darkness. For some, with good reason, this meant rushing home before night fell in order to seek safety. For others this meant opening up homes and firing up grills to share some food and resources with neighbors. The void is not always darkness, but also lack of resources—that which is absent—where those who survived the Hurricane made what they needed with what they had, and then some.[123]

My collaborators often mentioned how hope eradicated their fear of acting. Many external and internal factors limit how far our hopes are embodied in practice. Fear is one of them, and although my focus here is on imagination and memories, fear of the unknown—of this void—limits the ways we allow ourselves to participate in movements. In his *Politics of Fear, Practices of Hope*, theologian Stephen Skrimshire argues that "politics of fear discipline the body."[124] Colonialism, an example of a politic of fear, tries to fill this void with a narrative, a *cuento*, that assures its hearers that there is nothing beyond the threshold of that void. It says that political independence for Puerto Rico is impossible and detrimental to its future. The colonial *cuento* makes sure that systems are in place in order to make this *cuento* come true. But Skrimshire argues that "bodies that enable a culture of hope . . . are powerful when they expose as illusory the everyday reasons by which people need *not* be in solidarity."[125]

Despite the small sample size, the six congregations I collaborated with have much in common with most of the other 6,000-plus churches on the island. Because they mostly vacillate between conservative and moderate, they have similar practices including (lack of) inclusion of LGBTQIA folks and other religious cultures. However, something else these six congregations had in common—and I would like to believe that they shared this with the rest of the island's congregations post-María—is their demonstration of solidarity through a ministry of compassion, which was their embodied practice of hope. As mentioned in previous chapters, the crisis of María created collisions of congregations who set out to manifest their call of service to all. Helping people under these circumstances was a matter of life or death, and these congregations chose life.

There is no need to maintain the sense of harrowing crisis and anxiety that followed the storm in order to offer hope. But it is important to sustain and maintain the sense of immediacy of the church needing to reach *all* in the community in order to serve and fulfill spiritual and material needs. As Skrimshire asks, how are these acts of compassion and solidarity performed in ways that dismantle the illusion of their impossibility? For theologian Bryan Stone, "The hope of compassion . . . is a positive and quite 'earthy' hope that in and through the experience of compassionate community with victims, liberation is possible—here and now, in our time and in our place."[126] Stone articulates that compassion happens in community, specifically the Christian community, as a way of living together.[127]

A "compassionate community with victims" is not intended to mean a paternalistic ministry. Nor does a community need to prove who qualifies as a victim. According to Albert Memmi, we are all victims of colonization, and sooner or later we will all be victims of climate change, if we are not already. That said, it is important for the language of victimhood not to flatten oppression and suffering by falling into the problematics of the chant "All Lives Matter," for example. For Jon Sobrino, the action of God's love is compassion. It is an action driven by the suffering of the other that has reached one's heart and gut (*tripas y corazón*), and a complete human person is one who feels the other's suffering.[128]

Practices of hope through sustained solidarity and compassion can deliver us from evil (Empire) and keep us in the world (life), because they force the Christian community to think outside of its socially imposed limitations; *sin miedo, pa'encima*. Encountering people in need in the passing of Hurricane María forced those who were oblivious to the needs of their communities to act beyond their means and to sustain that practice. There is no *one* way to practice hope. The practice of hope takes the shape of what it needs: education, political and civic participation, community building, resistance, and survival. It is the guts that makes the hearts, *de tripas corazones*. For Fluker, as with Alves, "hope is born of the acknowledgement of the tragic character of human existence, yet it refuses to give up."[129] Or, as the Spanish expression goes, "*Armarse de valor*."[130] *Valor* translates as both "value" and "courage." This expression encourages its hearers to prepare themselves and take risks. I am not very keen on military language but to be *en la lucha* is also to fight, to continue pushing against something that is pushing against you. Clothing yourself with courage and value, in the context of decolonial practices of hope, means to remember your value and sense of agency. A decolonial practice of hope necessitates community, to piece the memories together and to enact agency when others might not have it. It is a communal *empuje* (push/trust) that dives into and calls out from the void with a hope that a new creation will emerge.

CONCLUSION

Hope, and/or hopelessness, gives us a metanarrative, a concrete ground to stand on. The things that we hope for, or stopped hoping for, show what our faith is and towards where we move. The hopes of a church community, and where these hopes are placed, trace the trajectory of where hope will take them. In the local congregations that collaborated with me there is a tug between hope and hopelessness, a momentum of defining and understanding their elasticity of hope as a community.

One collaborator lamented how "*tenemos una generación completa [en Puerto Rico] que va a seguir viviendo en este espejismo de supuesta estabilidad y aun el asunto de estatus no se ha resuelto.*"[131] Two others mentioned how many people in their congregation did not move to the United States, but only because their churches sustained them.[132] Another collaborator mentioned the finale performance at a 2018 denominational conference. When the singers brought out a giant Puerto Rican flag that basically covered everyone on the stage, they said, "*Y yo me sentí como si en aquel momento estuviéramos siendo bautizados en una nueva realidad, que es una realidad no solamente socioeconómica y política, es una realidad espiritual también.*"[133]

Theologian Juan Luis Segundo speaks about liberation as anxiety-producing—not despair—and the Christian church as having to be open to creativity, the creativity that produces liberation.[134] Liberation—political, historical, spatial, and embodied—is a matter of life or death for Puerto Rico. Maybe without liberation it will be a slow death, but it will be an unnatural death none the less, not a death that produces resurrection or a death that is part of life.¹³⁵ Life seems like it continues to function every day thanks to a stagnant *cuento* of impossibilities and dehumanization. *Vivir del cuento* does not sustain any life anymore.

Law and political theorist Elena Loiziduo says "that dreaming is an essential element of our political subjectivity."¹³⁶ As mentioned in chapter 3, the concern at this point is not a mere survival of the human race, but how to prevent the most vulnerable from perishing due to their oppression. Practices of hope embolden people and communities to live into their imaginations, pursuing dreams, jumping into the void with hope for creation instead of living out of tall tales. Theologian Keri Day, when speaking about radicalized hope through activism, argues that hope's precondition is despair and darkness.¹³⁷ She says, "Radical hope offers the conditions that give rise to alternative social worlds out of which beloved communities can emerge and flourish."¹³⁸ Day's argument affirms chapter 2's argument, where hope is not at the end but at the center of what pushes people forward towards participation in community. In chapter 5, I will show how the concepts discussed in this book so far (memory, decoloniality, political participation, liberation, and hope) work together to create a formula for a hope that is sustainable and aims toward liberation.

Chapter Five

About Telos: "Más Largo que la Esperanza del Pobre"

Más largo que la esperanza del pobre ("longer than the hope of the poor") is a phrase used when something seems never-ending and/or long-lasting. It is usually employed to indicate defeat, because that for which the poor person hopes never comes. So, this saying might not be the best example of an uplifting conclusion! This may seem like the kind of hope that would keep the marginalized from realizing a freedom from their oppression. However, the phrase also draws attention to the reality that scarcity does not have to mean hopelessness. This expression is especially poignant if we continue to follow Rubem Alves's argument that the ones who should envision their freedom are the oppressed themselves, because they are the ones who know what is missing. It means that action needs to spring from the hope of the poor and marginalized.

The research herein is meant to be taken as a whole. Chapter 1 argued the need to end the evil of colonization and unsustainable socio-economic practices, employing the colloquial saying *"no hay mal que dure cien años, ni cuerpo que lo resista."* Here, I proposed liberation and decolonization to bring about the end of this evil, for neither our bodies nor the promise of a hopeful future can withstand it anymore. Throughout, I have sought to understand this *mal* (evil), weaving back and forth between naming and describing evil in the Puerto Rican context, on one hand, while seeking out and arguing what our hope is and should be, what hope is made from, and what challenges hope and hoping face in that context on the other hand. Chapter 2 built a theoretical understanding of hope that can impact practices influenced by people's way of hoping, presenting concepts that challenge hope, such as optimism and hopelessness, through the work of Rubem Alves, Ellen Ott Marshall, and Jürgen Moltmann, among others. Chapter 3 attempted to rethink ecclesiology in conversation with qualitative research that helps frame and illustrate practices of hope in the context of post–María Puerto Rico. Finally, chapter

4 offered a theoretical discussion of collective memory, postcolonial and decolonizing theologies, and liberation theologies, seeking to articulate their importance for constructing a sustainable hope.

In this final chapter, I present a model for hope through a hermeneutics of liberation that is meant to be seen as one alternative and not as the exhaustion of all possibilities.[1] This model of hope is twofold. First it will illustrate how hope is an axis. Then from all the data collected through this research, and feeding from the first model, I propose a recipe for sustainable hope as a second model. I will present my conclusions, as I have done throughout, from a practical theological lens, as well as by accentuating the liberative epistemological and practical aspects of hope. As an example of this recipe model, I will further develop what the contours of a *proyecto de país* might look like, drawing on the theoretical analysis of previous chapters and what I gathered through my interviews. It is a recipe because as a model it is limited and shaped by context. A recipe asks for basic ingredients, which I will illustrate, but the flavors and additions will vary from context to context. It is a recipe because it searches for a result but at the same time allows for the possibility of change.

Memory, I argued in chapter 4, feeds into our ways of knowing, which in turn flows into our actions that comprise the political sphere. All memories are shaped by the systems structuring reality in our society, systems like colonization, Christianity, and capitalism, which ultimately define our hopes and shape our imaginations and ideas for liberation. Memory influences the things that we hope for and how we hope. I have also shown how these themes and claims can relate to contexts outside the Puerto Rican context. However, Puerto Rican hope is related to who Puerto Ricans are. This is not to say that Puerto Rican hope is derived from Puerto Rican opinion; rather, it is intrinsically related to the subjectivities that entail being Puerto Rican, which is why the themes of colonization and political freedom are so important in my articulation. I agree here with Teresa Delgado who argues that Puerto Rican subjectivity transcends its historical context in the ways it can influence and shape decolonial theology. She says, referring to Puerto Ricans, "The story of our people has a profound effect on our ability to do justice in the world."[2]

In chapter 1, I alluded to markers that help distinguish a hope that is sustainable and liberative. With the exception of the final question, a hope that is sustainable answers the following questions affirmatively: Does ecclesial practice, production, or discourse denote an expectation for the future? What does it expect? Does the discourse of hope understand and take into account material reality? Does it model a pedagogy of solidarity? Does it foster liberation, imagination, and flourishing? Can this hope be shared across social and religious divisions? Is the practice of hope in question, harmful, or oppressive?

A sustainable hope is twofold. First, if hope is sustainable this means that it is a hope that accounts for what nurtures and hinders hope simultaneously in order for it to be maintained (sustained) and passed on as that toward which we are all working. And it is also a hope that is able to sustain practices. One question arising from my interviews, and frequently raised in this book, is how we can continue to practice hope when people start losing interest in participation and energies toward change diminish. The question of how to sustain practices relates to the values with which our hopes are infused.

These questions (markers), although they do not exhaust the ways one can get at sustainable hope, are meant as a guide for discerning where hope exists and what it might look like. First, they show what a hope or practice of hope expects, so as to be clear about why the church engages in particular practices and perhaps to discern whether they need revision as a means of walking towards what is expected. Second, they investigate whether a discourse on hope accounts for the realities and material conditions of individuals and society. Hope expects the "not yet" and invites imagination; however, if hope invites people's present actions but does not take into consideration our material realities, it can be a source of oppression, not of liberation. This is why hope asks for a pedagogy of solidarity that shows whether practices are harmful, oppressive, or excluding of others and nature. Paulo Freire's pedagogy of solidarity asks how solidarity looks in the classroom and how a pedagogical worldview contributes to this. Freire, before formally speaking about education, describes human nature as a process of becoming. He understands that the need for education comes from our incompleteness, our constant becoming, as unique to the human condition. In this process, as education comes into play regardless of the content of the class, Freire suggests the need for a set of questions. Even when he is teaching Portuguese grammar or math, he says:

> [. . .] I must also know in favor of what, in favor of whom, in favor of what dream am I teaching [. . .]As a consequence of thinking in favor of whom, in favor of what, in favor of what dream I am teaching I will have to think against whom, against what, against what dream I am teaching.[3]

Our practices are informed by our discourses and beliefs, which are geared towards somewhere. Hope, influenced by a pedagogy of solidarity, helps us to be aware of those who are outside of our communication communities.

Finally, these questions account for an eschatology that fosters liberation, imagination, and flourishing. Taking into consideration Ellen Ott Marshall's sense of hope as elastic, where hope keeps the tensions of promise and peril, means that hope accounts for present material conditions at the same time that we account for the "not yet."[4]

MODELS OF HOPE

Teresa Delgado believes "Blessed are those who continue to hope beyond hope, for they shall be called architects of a free and joyful life."[5] This section will suggest two ways of systematizing hope in models. The understanding of the axis model builds and directly affects the recipe model. In other words, the ways hope as axis is influenced and shaped by its context (exterior elements) will change the recipe for a sustainable hope. The first model helps to visually represent hope as ontological: what hope is made of and what influences it, as axis. The second model helps to visually represent sustainable hope, as recipe. In the final section of this chapter, I argue for a *proyecto de país* that is shaped by my research findings and by a theory of sustainable hope.

About Telos: "Más Largo que la Esperanza del Pobre" 105

MODEL FOR HOPE: AXIS

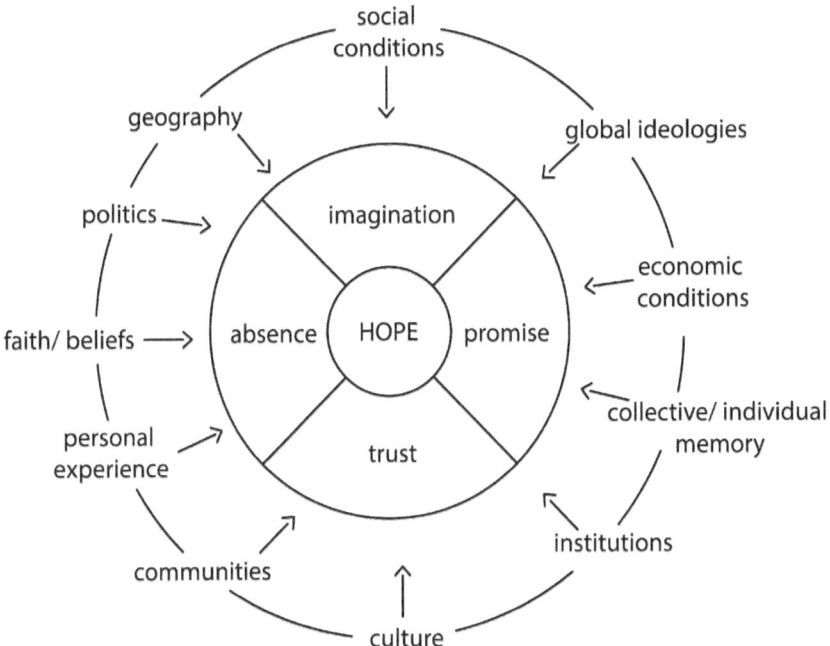

Figure 5.1 Hope Axis Model Inward
Source: Created by author.

The first model (F5.1) is influenced by the analysis of hope throughout my book and by the ways hope has been put in dialogue with other disciplines. In chapter 1, I mentioned that hope's centrality makes it function as an axis, as this imaginary line around which our actions and practices rotate. This diagram shows how hope is built and how hope can function as it moves. Over the course of this book I have argued for a holistic sense of hope by bringing together the elements that make and shape hope, noted in the first model. Continuing chapter 2's argument that the capacity to hope is ontological, this model puts hope at the center of what motivates our actions. Hope is not an afterthought; it is centralized because it nurtures what some people do and how they are in the world. This diagram pictures the building blocks of hope as imagination, promise, absence, and trust. Lack of hope is lack of imagination; there is a direct correlation between hoping and our ability to imagine what lies beyond, or a different future than what the present portends. The imagined fills out the void, that which is absent from our present and that we hope to attain in our future. The ability to wait in hope and believe in the promise—promise used here as "that which is hoped for"—comes from trust in whatever external or internal force, system, or entity will enable the path of hope.

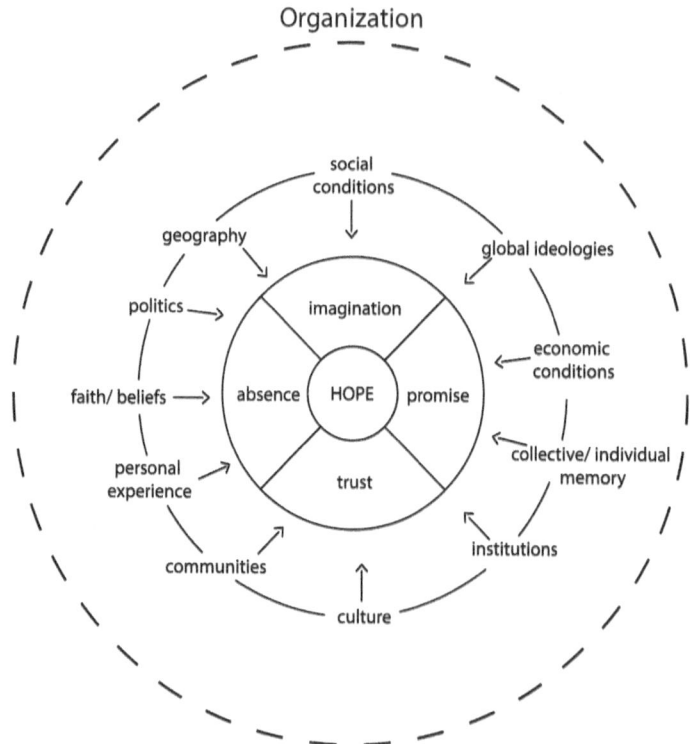

Figure 5.2 Hope Axis Model Organization
Source: Created by author.

The categories surrounding hope are some of the external agents, as the arrows indicate, informing hope: *global ideologies* that arrange society (colonialism, capitalism, socialism, neoliberalism, etc.), *economic conditions* (wealth, poverty, debt, access to economic benefits), *collective/individual memory* (popular wisdom, stories, history), *institutions* (education entities, churches, government, market, media), *culture* (social constructions, sexualities, class, gender, race, customs), *communities* (family, friends, networks), *personal experiences* (events, biological/emotional/psycho/social health conditions), *faith and/or belief* (religious systems, spiritualities, morals, values), *politics* (public policy, legal system), *geography* (place, ecology, natural environment), and *social conditions* (access to social resources, safety/security, health care). These categories are interconnected in more ways than one.

Some are subcategories of others. What they mean specifically depends on the context that informs them. For example, the global ideology overarching society's government model influences economic conditions. Capitalism, for instance, impacts the ways governments are structured and communities are organized, influencing individuals' economic condition. These categories are society's *Organizations* (F5.2), Alves's term for the ways we organize society.[6] The circle for Organization in figure F.2 is made from interrupted segments to signify that these strategies for organizing, although they give the illusion of absolutism, are constructions and therefore open to change.

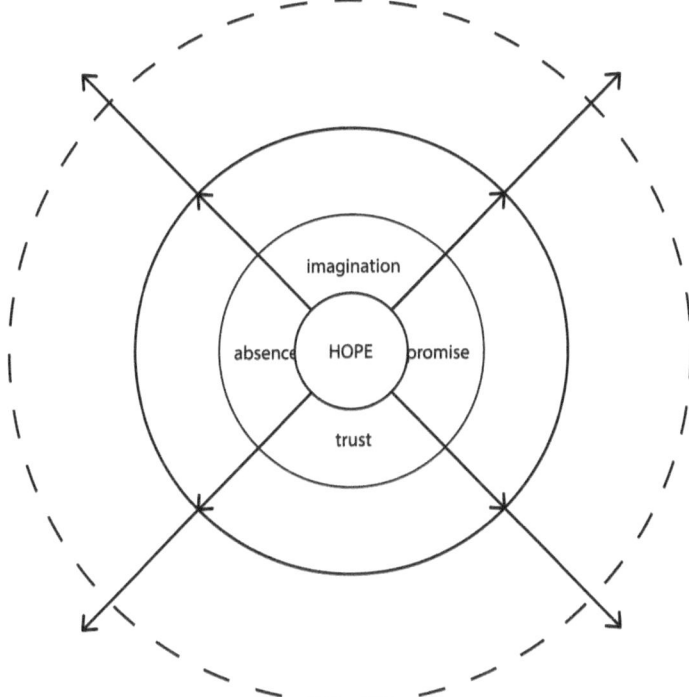

Figure 5.3 Hope Axis Model Outward

Figure F5.3 visualizes how hope pushes outward into particular areas of society, to the limits of Organization and/or beyond it. This model, composed of these three figures, is a simple two-dimensional, symmetric, and presumably equal way of depicting hope. However, to better envision hope, we should imagine that there is movement and layering within Organizations and that, in reality, they are not influencing each other in equal amounts, just as the center of hope's components are not necessarily influencing each other in equal amounts. For example, in some forms of hope absence can be greater than imagination and promise, shaping and cultivating hope differently than if imagination were predominant. Sometimes Organizations also impact hope at different levels. The purpose of this model, however, is not to cover all the ways Organization interacts with hope and hope's components, but to give visual guidance for understanding hope's complexity and movement as hope is constantly being revised. With Marshall's concept of elasticity, this model helps us to understand how hope is constantly in flux, influenced by the ways society and Organization affects it, and as its axis, though always at the center, expands and/or shrinks.

Model for Sustainable Hope

The second model, in the form of a recipe, is influenced by the first model in conversation with my analysis of how to make hope sustainable through practice. The first model presents a generalized understanding of what hope is and how it functions and serves as the premise for my next model. This second model is more refined in the sense that it has a specific *telos*, a specific outcome of a hope that is sustainable and liberative. (Op + I + So) CW = SH expresses the ingredients: (Oppression Perspective + Imagination + Solidarity) Collective Work = Practice of Sustainable Hope. A combination of those elements enacts practices of hope. This recipe also represents an intentional way of hoping.

Without idealizing (OP) *Oppression Perspective*, or suffering, the oppressed are the first ingredient in this model because those who are oppressed are those who are not accommodated by the present conditions and can identify what is missing in order to stop suffering and oppression. This missing element gives us something to wait for or walk toward. Because hope is ontological, everyone has the *empuje* (push) of hoping. Those who do not experience oppression hope for the continuation of things as they are; the un-oppressed might rely more on optimism than on hope.

Hope is something we cannot physically see but can only imagine. If we are seeing hope (experiencing the realized hope), it has become reality. (I) *Imagination*, which holds the/a promise of a future, is the engine that shows that there are other ways of organizing and being, although it does not always show us exactly what those ways would be or how to achieve them. Imagination also holds the trust of its beliefs and cosmologies in order to envision transcendence towards a future. As imagination can run loose into a self-serving world, (So) *Solidarity* and compassion are key elements that require us to understand ourselves in relationship to others in ways that keep us from oppressing others.

The sum of these components, multiplied by (CW) *Collective Work*, generates a sustainable and liberative hope. Hope is enhanced by collective work because the greater it is, the more expansive hope can be. Collective Work implies that through action and community there is also change—change in present conditions but also change in the ways we expand and understand the elements inside the parentheses, because collectivity is informing the individual embodiments of oppression, imagination, and solidarity. Together these elements create a practice of (SH) *Sustainable Hope*, because the work and its articulation foster practices of solidarity, collectivity, and imagination. It is also sustainable because it depends on all of these elements to maintain a balance that, as it morphs, corrects and revises itself through an open process. This arrangement is an intentional way of being through hoping as a community. It is not a model exclusive to the church, but ecclesial practices can promote such a model through theology and education. In many cases, it is the hope that many congregations already practice at different scales (as noted in my interviews), just as it is a hope that awaits the flourishing of creation at the same times that it lives into creation in the present.

This model does not account for an explicit framework of interpretation of promise and peril because it abstracts the concepts and is articulated without the context, though it is not aiming at utopia. Solidarity, a hermeneutics of liberation, and community shape the ways in which one interprets what the hope is and where the hope is placed. The *telos* of a liberative practice as its outcome is just that: its aim. This is not to collapse or say that liberation is unattainable, but to understand that it is always becoming as context continues to influence it. Take the abolition of slavery, for example, as a practice of hopeful liberation that happened in reality. Nonetheless, we continue to struggle against its remains as well as against new ways of slavery. For millennia, "progress" has been achieved through slavery and the exploitation of humans and natural resources. Less than two hundred years after it has been abolished in the United States and other parts of the world, capitalism seeks to find new forms of slavery instead of new forms of fair production. Political advancement and economic development are still predicated on the principle of slavery.[7] A model of hope must take these realities into account.

In one of his most famous passages, citing his friend Fernando Birri, Uruguayan writer Eduardo Galeano says, "*[La utopia] está en el horizonte. Me acerco dos pasos, ella se aleja dos pasos. Camino diez pasos y el horizonte se corre diez pasos más allá. Por mucho que yo camine, nunca la alcanzaré. ¿Para qué sirve la utopía? Para eso sirve: para caminar.*"[8] The movement towards a liberative hope directs society, or in this case, churches in Puerto Rico. Again, as Alves writes, "The petty triumphs of the individual are no sign of hope to those who remain entrapped."[9] Communities that are predicated on "serving thy neighbor" and love for others, such as the

Christian church, necessitate an analysis of how their hopes are professed and practiced. Rubem Alves and Juan Luis Segundo both believe the church is the optimal place for the coexistence of patience (that waits on hope) and urgency (of hope to be put in motion).

For a century, "hope" in Puerto Rico has often meant leaving the island, primarily in the direction of the United States. In the face of such constant crisis, I wondered what people held on to and what the church was offering as hope. This is why my project searched for practices of hope in order to identify what hope looks like to people living in Puerto Rico today. However, it does not assume work, participation, and loyalties toward a sustainable hope is limited to those on the island. In the next section, I propose an example of the bedrock of what hope can look like, using the models of hope to envision a *proyecto de país* with an ecclesial and theological lens. By establishing the scope of this proposal as a national endeavor, it assumes the search for public and political strategies and platforms to practice hope.

PROYECTO DE PAÍS

The idea for a *proyecto de país* that would envision a future for Puerto Rico and an understanding of the commitment of the Puerto Rican church to larger society sprouted from my project interviews. According my collaborators, there is a persistent lack of dialogue between the church and organizations outside the ecclesial sphere. A *proyecto de país* argues for a systemic ecclesial approach to other institutions and forms of civic participation that are able to attend to the source of problems and not their symptoms. For example, although the work of some local churches is to feed the hungry neighboring the congregation, it is also important to understand how can this be approached in a way that changes not only the conditions of the individual but also the means that create the conditions.

A *proyecto de país* ought to consider the importance of the separation of church and state, so it does not propose a Christian government. Eighteen of my nineteen collaborators mentioned the importance of this separation. This is particularly true since my research does not include non-Christian voices whose traditions and cosmologies would shape this project differently. My aim, in fact, is to politically decentralize the Christian church so that it does not lose its prophetic voice. In following the *(OP + I + So) CW = SH* model as its principle, a *proyecto de país* as an ecclesial mission might begin to look as follows:

Perspective of Oppression. This ingredient is the recovery of historical abuse and exploitation through the means of colonization, disaster capitalism, racism, sexism, and religiosity, and the articulation of how this suffering and oppression look under present systems and practices; assessing who is being represented in the church's decision-making; and if work for the "needy" is based on assumptions about or in conversations with those served. This lens assesses the people or structures who have power and asks how power is distributed or exuded. In the context of Puerto Rico, more specifically, envisioning a sustainable hope must include and invite the perspective of churches that serve poor communities. Pastor and theologian Jules Martínez, while reflecting on aid and response after Hurricane María, noticed that the congregations that were serving poor and hard-to-access communities were the Pentecostal churches. The rate of response and communal outreach was greater for these congregations than for bigger institutions and mainline denominations.[10]

This ingredient also calls forward the analysis of memory and decolonization from chapter 4. Nora relates an increased interest in memory studies to an acceleration of history: the world is rapidly and continuously changing. Meanwhile, new practices of unearthing memories from minority groups have emerged.[11] He attributes this to three types of memory decolonization. First, "international decolonization" has allowed a new process of recognizing the fabrications of colonial memories. Second, "domestic decolonization" has recognized and integrated minority memories into the Western "mainstream" narrative and identified the particularity of each community. Third, "ideological decolonization" is the reunification of "these liberated peoples" with destroyed memories.[12] I am not proposing a quest for a "pure" memory or historical account that reveals the Truth, but rather a search that will expand communities of communication, both ideological and material communities. This will make people aware of who and what is not accounted for in the search for liberation and just practices.

Imagination in a *proyecto de país* is the capacity of the individual and community to imagine through what emerges from their dreams, beliefs, and projections of a future. Imagination also means to allow oneself to play, as Rubem Alves suggests and as I discussed in chapter 2. Imagination is the capacity to remember the malleability of structures and systems as they have been constructed and can be reconstructed. To play means to remember that when something is not working anymore or has met its expiration date, new things can be created.[13] Puerto Rico's current political status as a territory of the United States and its history of colonization has created systems of oppression that make people think that there is no way out towards a more just future, especially without the United States' protection.[14] These claims of inferiority and incapability become petrified in the imagination of Puerto Ricans. Play and imagination help expand or shatter the walls from political and economic restraint of the United States. Luis Rivera Pagán says, *"El desafío de las iglesias evangélicas* [en Puerto Rico] *y sus pensadores teológicos es propiciar, mediante sus facultades creadoras, del cultivo, y evolución de ese proceso* [de unificación e identidad nacional] *asumiéndolo como proyecto de una nacionalidad caribeña y latinoamericana más libre y justa."*[15]

When telling a story, either real or fictitious—mostly gossip—people begin with the expression *"imagínate."* An accurate interpretation in English is "picture it." However, a literal translation is "imagine yourself." This opening invites the listener not only to picture the situation but to imagine themselves in it. This expression is also what children typically say to each other when they are about to invite a friend into their imaginative world so they can play together. Imagination invites people to imagine themselves and/or their communities as part of a different reality. It can be a communal practice as people invite others to share their visions, making room for other possibilities as others imagine themselves in them.

Solidarity exhorts the churches to look at the ways they preach and practice relationships. Solidarity looks at with whom and how the church invests time and resources. Solidarity assesses a church's inclusion and means of compassion through its practices. For example, the church assesses who it has been called to be with and looks for the best practices to stand with them. Solidarity, especially using Isasi-Díaz's definition, is not a paternalistic or hierarchical approach but seeks to live with and walk alongside people rather than prescribe solutions or become people's savior. According to Alves, "the price of fellowship which does not grow out of the true alliance of the heart is hypocrisy. This is one of the dramas of ecumenism. It wants to create unity by institutional gimmicks—overlooking the fact that community has to grow out of life."[16]

In Chapter 3, I mentioned that my collaborators realized the importance of ecumenism, as well as their lack of success in this endeavor. The work of Hurricane María forced people to walk, be, and work in solidarity with all the people they encountered, regardless of religious and social differences. One collaborator mentioned how one of the homes they visited with their congregation to offer help was that of a same-sex couple. The doctrinal convictions of this collaborator did not interfere with offering necessary resources. Furthermore, the collaborator reflected on this encounter and wondered how this couple had experienced the church in that moment and how this collaborator might have had taken indirect part in their oppression previous to this encounter. Solidarity also exists in ties and relationships between islanders and the diaspora. Therefore, solidarity is not limited to space but is inclusive of the body. Solidarity asks the question, Who is the Puerto Rican body? And it answers that question expansively rather than narrowly.

Collaborative Work is the integration of communal work and partnership with movements, initiatives, and/or organizations. All of the previous ingredients (oppression, imagination, and solidarity) work together as they inform each other. They are then amplified and put into work in collaborative practices. These practices happen within the local congregation, between the local congregation and surrounding community, and in the interaction of the local congregation with other communities beyond their neighboring communities. It keeps practices in movement and flux. The work the churches began to do collectively after Hurricane María is a good example of the ways the expansion of collective work, with a commitment to solidarity, imagination, and standing with the suffering and oppressed, came to be. Collaborative work is generated from the desire—in this case the desire of the church—to be present in the world and engage in public and political theology. In order for it to generate sustainable hope and avoid reproducing oppressive practices, it needs to be accompanied by the voice of the oppressed, imagination, and solidarity.

Sustainable Hope is a hope that can be sustained and remain sustaining by accounting for the material conditions as well as the Divine, or trust in the future. *(OP + I + So) CW = SH*: the outcome of this recipe is a practice of sustainable hope. It is sustainable because, as the elements work together, they work toward expansion and inclusion, keeping hope alive. It is work done intentionally to offer a response to the material needs of people as well as a nurturing of *la facultad* and the ontological character of hope. Furthermore, it is a hope that encourages and thrives on creation.

A *proyecto de país* can have several stages. I am proposing a first stage in which the *proyecto* is not a political platform but a guide for the body of the church to articulate how it will relate to society and its material needs and conditions as principles. In order for it to become a political platform, the *proyecto* needs to first feed congregations as a model for engaging society and gaining the trust of larger society. As mentioned in Chapter 4, the church has *poder de convocatoria;* establishing a *proyecto de país* would give the ecclesial institution a map that helps hone that power. Denominations, as governing bodies, would draft a detailed articulation of what their mission is for Puerto Rico, including their political aspirations —political as in public policy. It would be helpful for these documents to be publicly available. The congregations that participated in my project have no such documents accessible. The second stage of a *proyecto de país* would propose specific solutions and strategies to address the issues of Organizations. Finally, a third stage would look for ways to implement the *proyecto*.

Again, this *proyecto* is tied to practices of sustainable hope, accounting for the inclusion of all peoples in solidarity. It is not the expansion of a personal or small-group agenda but of the work that has been done collectively for the community trusting that the Spirit weaves together the intentions of the people who leave themselves to be met by her. As argued in Chapter 3, the Holy Spirit plays an important role in the life of the church as the initiator of change and possibilities. A sensitivity to this Divine being allows for a *proyecto de país* to be woven in one spirit, regardless of its multifaceted shape.

To summarize, a *proyecto de país* for the church in Puerto Rico is inclusive, participatory, conscious, other serving, decolonial, and public. Thus, it responds to three of the four practices of hope the collaborators alluded to in Chapter 3: (1) being prophetic (public participation and annunciation); (2) being coherent (building trust with the church and larger society); and (3) being the hope (embodying practices that point to the hope). *Mejor malo conocido que bueno por conocer* is another common expression in Spanish, translating to "the evil known is better than the good to be known." It projects the fear of the unknown, regardless of the promise of better conditions. Its use reflects that the person has settled because they managed to survive the current evil. It also reflects the imaginary that explains why sometimes people do not engage in collective action and remain stagnant even under objectively bad conditions. The modeling of a church that resists stagnation under evil is the path toward hope.

"To have a plan" was the fourth practice to which my collaborators alluded. Though these models can converse with and inform other contexts, they are the product of the analysis of the Puerto Rican context practices of hope might look different elsewhere. In chapter 2, I described Rubem Alves's metaphor of birthing and conceiving hope for discerning context in order to understand what society is ready for. Elaborating a plan, in this case a *proyecto de país* in Puerto Rico, begins with the process of conceiving hope. This conception is, at least in part, what I have attempted in this book. The birthing of this hope would be the work and practice of this *proyecto* and one way of hoping sustainably.

CONCLUSION

When I set out to research this book my main questions were: What is hope? Where is it? What does it look like? I have isolated the concept of hope, but hope does not work alone. The thematic movement of each chapter (context, hope, practice, imagination, and aim) has led me to a model of hope constructed by the hope I found in ecclesial practices that appear to foster society's flourishing through solidarity and compassion. But the church, as an existing and incorporated institution, does not exhaust the ways in which Christian hope is practiced. As Collaborator #1 said, even if the insititutional churches are depleted, *"del pueblo mismo van a surgir experiencias de fe que va hacer que la iglesia continúe."*[17] Hope persists and transcends current structures, especially when these are no longer fostering liberation. Although the church as an institutional component of Organization still serves a purpose in Puerto Rico, hope does not exist because of the institution itself but because of the people who nurture it, or do not. Theologians like Leonardo Boff and George "Tink" Tinker have followed their hopes outside of the Christian church and beyond mainline religious institutions. After leaving the Franciscan Order, Boff wrote that he would continue on his path of hope, saying, "I have changed. Not the battle itself, but the trenches from which I shall fight."[18] The challenge of sustainable hope is to unearth what is at stake and build practices that will sustain a dignified life for all creation. The challenge to the institutional church is to listen to the faith that emerges from the people, not only to stay relevant, but so it can continue to be hope. *Más largo que la esperanza del pobre* centers the power of hope on those who are at the margins, those who know what is missing. A recipe that centers the hopes of the margins to foster something that can sustain peoples' lives and nature's flourishing requires imagining that there is something beyond what our circumstances reveal and breaks through the concrete that is suffocating what lies beneath. Hope is an ontological virtue that predisposes an expectation of the future. It is our walk both/and our wait on the things that have yet to materialize. It projects that which is yet to happen. A sustainable hope provides the means to materialize a hope in practice.

Notes

CHAPTER ONE

1. Although I did not come across recently published empirical studies that trace this sentiment of hopelessness, many political and academic popular writers point to and address a collective sense of hopelessness in their works. See, for example, "Vargas Vidot instruye la esperanza para las transformaciones," *Iniciativa Comunitaria* (blog), accessed June 4, 2018, http://www.iniciativacomunitaria.org/vargas-vidot-instruye-la-esperanza-para-las-transformaciones/; Joel Cintrón Arbasetti y Carla Minet, "Puerto Rico en crisis: panorámica de la sociedad civil," *Centro de Periodismo Investigativo*, accessed June 4, 2018, http://periodismoinvestigativo.com/2015/09/puerto-rico-en-crisis-panoramica-de-la-sociedad-civil/. One factor that can be used to assess the matter of hopelessness is the increase in suicide attempts and suicide statistics. See Caitlin Dickerson, "After Hurricane, Signs of a Mental Health Crisis Haunt Puerto Rico," *The New York Times*, January 20, 2018, accessed June 12, 2018, https://www.nytimes.com/2017/11/13/us/puerto-rico-hurricane-maria-mental-health.html; Amanda Holpuch, "Despair and Anxiety: Puerto Rico's 'living Emergency' as a Mental Health Crisis Unfolds," *The Guardian*, August 7, 2018, accessed August 24, 2018, http://www.theguardian.com/world/2018/aug/07/despair-and-anxiety-puerto-ricos-living-emergency-as-a-mental-health-crisis-unfolds.

2. When I use the term "Puerto Ricans" I am including the Puerto Rican Islanders and Puerto Rican Diaspora unless otherwise specified. By 2013 there were over five million Puerto Ricans in the United States, and the numbers continue to increase; see Gustavo López and Eileen Patten, "Hispanics of Puerto Rican Origin in the United States, 2013," Pew Research Center's Hispanic Trends Project, September 15, 2015, accessed June 12, 2018, http://www.pewhispanic.org/2015/09/15/hispanics-of-puerto-rican-origin-in-the-united-states-2013/. On the island of Puerto Rico, the 2010 Census showed that 63 percent of immigrants came from the United States, 20 percent come from the Dominican Republic, 5 percent come from Cuba, and 12 percent from elsewhere (Spain, Colombia, Mexico, Venezuela, Panama, Argentina, Germany, China, Peru, and Ecuador) (Luz E León, "La Población Inmigrante en Puerto Rico,"

Oficina de Estadísticas Gobierno de Puerto Rico, November 15, 2013, accessed June 24, 2018, http://www.estadisticas.gobierno.pr/iepr/LinkClick.aspx?fileticket =3OJ8yIPDQEU%3D).

3. Tax exemptions for foreign investors and relocated to the island displacing islanders and gentrifying the economy. See Law 20 and 22 of the Puerto Rico Civil code.

4. The Spaniards baptized the island of Borikén as the island of San Juan Bautista and its main port as Puerto Rico. Over the years these names changed and the island became known as Puerto Rico and its main port as San Juan. When the U.S. gained control, it changed that name to Porto Rico. It changed back to Puerto Rico in 1932 after congregational resolution (César J. Ayala and Rafael Bernabe, *Puerto Rico en el Siglo Americano: Su Historia desde 1898* [San Juan, PR: Ediciones Callejón, 2016], 120).

5. Ayala and Bernabe, *Puerto Rico en el Siglo Americano*, 31.

6. An example of this is depicted on a newspaper of the time, where it shows Uncle Sam in a classroom that showed the casts of society and in one interactions in the drawing he is admonishing four children and each had a ribbon that indicated their place of origin as "Philippines, Hawaii, Porto Rico, and Cuba." The blackboard reads: "The consent of the governed is a good thing in theory, but very rare in fact. England has governed her colonies whether they consented or not. By not waiting for their consent she has greatly advanced the world's civilization. The U.S. must govern its new territories with or without their consent until they can govern themselves." Louis Darlympe. *School Begins*, 1899. http://www.loc.gov/pictures/item/2012647459/

7. Ayala and Bernabe, *Puerto Rico En El Siglo Americano*, 24–25.

8. A criollo is a person born in the Americas from Spanish parents (Ayala and Bernabe, *Puerto Rico en el Siglo Americano*, 43).

9. Ayala and Bernabe, *Puerto Rico En El Siglo Americano*, 31.

10. Ayala and Bernabe, *Puerto Rico En El Siglo Americano*, 31–37.

11. Languages like Spanish (estadounidense), French (états-unien), Portuguese (estadunidense), among others, offer a gerund for the people from the United States. I want to avoid using the term "American" since for many scholars, including myself, it is a contingent term that renders a continent invisible. See Eliseo Pérez Alvarez, *Abya Yala: Discursos Desde La América Des-Norteada* (Mexico City, Mexico: El Faro, 2010).

12. Ayala and Bernabe, *Puerto Rico En El Siglo Americano*, 43.

13. Ayala and Bernabe, *Puerto Rico En El Siglo Americano*, 43–44. Racism also exists in Puerto Rico and has marked the Puerto Rican culture as well as limited its growth and work for justice. See Ayala and Bernabe, *Puerto Rico En El Siglo Americano*, and José Luis González, *El País de Los Cuatro Pisos y Otros Ensayos* (Río Piedras, PR: Ediciones Huracán, 1985). See Jalil Suede Badillo and Angel Lopez Cantos, *Puerto Rico Negro* (San Juan: Editorial Cultural, 1986).

14. Ayala and Bernabe, *Puerto Rico En El Siglo Americano*, 47.

15. Déborah Berman Santana, "Puerto Rico's Operation Bootstrap: Colonial Roots of a Present Model for "Third World Development," *Revista Geográfica* 124 (January-December 1998): 100–101.

16. Ayala and Bernabe, *Puerto Rico En El Siglo Americano*, 42, 89.

17. This Act was amended thirty years later and allowed Puerto Ricans to elect their governor as well as to draft a Constitution for the island. Plantation capitalism term coined by James Lawson to describe the economic system in the United States.

18. Berman Santana, "Puerto Rico's Operation Bootstrap," 102. For an analysis on Puerto Rico's political status and proposal of an independent future, which the author calls a window towards hope, see Arturo Estrella, *Ventana a la Esperanza: Un Proyecto para Puerto Rico* (San Juan, PR: Editores Publicaciones Puertorriqueñas, 1996.)

19. Déborah Berman Santana, *Kicking Off the Bootstraps: Environment, Development, and Community Power in Puerto Rico* (Tucson, AZ: University of Arizona Press, 1996), 73.

20. Berman Santana, "Puerto Rico's Operation Bootstrap," 91.

21. Berman Santana, "Puerto Rico's Operation Bootstrap," 104.

22. Berman Santana, "Puerto Rico's Operation Bootstrap," 89.

23. Berman Santana, "Puerto Rico's Operation Bootstrap," 91.

24. Berman Santana, "Puerto Rico's Operation Bootstrap," 104. Fomento is the Puerto Rico Industrial Development Company; in Spanish, Compañía de Fomento Industrial de Puerto Rico.

25. Translation, put her first shoes on her feet.

26. Popular Democratic Party.

27. Berman Santana, "Puerto Rico's Operation Bootstrap," 93.

28. Berman Santana, "Puerto Rico's Operation Bootstrap," 94.

29. Nelson Álvarez Febles, "La agricultura ecológica puede producir alimentos para Puerto Rico," *80grados* (blog), January 27, 2012, accessed January 16, 2019, http://www.80grados.net/la-agricultura-ecologica-puede-producir-alimentos-para-puerto-rico/.

30. Teresa Delgado, *A Puerto Rican Decolonial Theology: Prophesy Freedom* (London: Palgrave Macmillan, 2017), 77.

31. Berman Santana, "Puerto Rico's Operation Bootstrap," 99.

32. El Nuevo Día, "Puerto Rico es el tercer país de mayor desigualdad económica en el mundo," *El Nuevo Día*, September 17, 2018, accessed January 14, 2019, https://www.elnuevodia.com/negocios/economia/nota/puertoricoeseltercerpaisdemayordesigualdadeconomicaenelmundo-2447734/.

33. I make the distinction between Puerto Ricans and island locals to account for the island's immigrant population. If I were to use only "Puerto Ricans," I would risk erasing the demographic diversity in the island.

34. Samuel Silva Gotay, *La Iglesia Católica de Puerto Rico En El Procesos Político de Americanización (1898–1930)* (San Juan, PR: Publicaciones Gaviota, 2012), 61–62.

35. Samuel Silva Gotay, "Desarrollo de La Dimensión Religiosa Del Nacionalismo En Puerto Rico: 1898–1989," *Estudios Interdisciplinarios de América Latina y El Caribe* 1, no. 1 (June 1990), NP.

36. Silva Gotay, *La Iglesia Católica de Puerto Rico*, 83. In *Dios o el Oro de las Indias*, Gustavo Gutiérrez explains how Todelo believes that the colonial process of

The Americas is a gift to Spain from God for its triumph over the war against the moors. Gustavo Gutiérrez, *Dios o el Oro de las Indias,* (Salamanca, España; Ediciones Sígueme, 1989), pp. 102–106.

37. "By making sacred the political processes of cultural, military imposition, and politics over Puerto Rico" (Silva Gotay, "Desarrollo de La Dimensión Religiosa Del Nacionalismo En Puerto Rico," 5, translation mine).

38. Silva Gotay, *La Iglesia Católica de Puerto Rico*, 78.

39. Silva Gotay, *La Iglesia Católica de Puerto Rico*, 194.

40. Silva Gotay, *La Iglesia Católica de Puerto Rico*, 198.

41. From Ponce. He participated in the Irish insurrection of 1916 which then influenced his aticulations of the independence party in Puerto Rico.

42. Following the annexation, Catholic clergy had to go through seminary in the United States to be priests in Puerto Rico (Silva Gotay, *La Iglesia Católica de Puerto Rico*, 300).

43. Samuel Silva Gotay, *Protestantismo y Política en Puerto Rico, 1898–1930: Hacia Una Historia Del Protestantismo Evangélico En Puerto Rico* (San Juan, PR: Editorial de la Universidad de Puerto Rico, 1998), 99.

44. Silva Gotay, *Protestantismo y Política En Puerto Rico,* 4.

45. Matt Egan, "Who Owns Puerto Rico's Mountain of Debt? You Do," *CNNMoney*, September 27, 2017, accessed June 24, 2018, http://money.cnn.com/2017/09/27/investing/puerto-rico-debt-who-owns-trump/index.html.

46. "As our population migrates and dies, millionaires will arrive doing business, buying and restoring buildings, mainly in the historical and touristic areas, thanks to the incentives of laws 20 and 21. The plan is not just to pay the bondholders. The agenda is to supplant the population with foreign millionaires and reduce us to a minority. No one will have any capital to return. Puerto Rico will cease to be an economic option for Puerto Ricans. The ones who stay will be the new servants. We will delight the new social class with our folkloric dances of *bomba*, *danza*, and *plena*. And yes, the bondholders will receive their pay at the same time that they annihilate us as people" (Fermín Arraiza, "El Plan Que Aniquilará Al Pueblo" *Periódico El Nuevo Día*, March 15, 2017, accessed June 14, 2018, https://www.elnuevodia.com/opinion/columnas/elplanqueaniquilaraalpueblo-columna-2300782/, translation mine).

47. José A. Delgado, "Jueza Taylor Swain mantiene la constitucionalidad de Promesa," *El Nuevo Dia*, July 13, 2018, accessed July 13, 2018, http://www.elnuevodia.com/noticias/tribunales/nota/juezataylorswainmantienelaconstitucionalidaddepromesa-2435003/. See also "La jueza Laura Taylor Swain celebra vista sobre el acuerdo de Cofina," *El Nuevo Dia*, January 16, 2019, accessed Januarry 16, 2019, https://www.elnuevodia.com/noticias/tribunales/nota/lajuezalaurataylorswaincelebravistasobreelacuerdodecofina-2471155/.

48. In English, the *Junta de Caridad* is the "Charity Council." See Silva Gotay, *La Iglesia Católica de Puerto Rico*, 80.

49. Silva Gotay, *La Iglesia Católica de Puerto Rico*, 231.

50. Silva Gotay, *La Iglesia Católica de Puerto Rico*, 233.

51. See Frances Robles, "FEMA Was Sorely Unprepared for Puerto Rico Hurricane, Report Says," *The New York Times*, July 14, 2018, accessed, July 18, 2018, https://www.nytimes.com/2018/07/12/us/fema-puerto-rico-maria.html.

52. "Much of the island was destroyed, with billions of dollars owed to Wall Street and the banks which, sadly, must be dealt with" (Bryan Logan, "Trump Tweets Puerto Rico Is 'in Deep Trouble' While the Country Struggles to Recover from Hurricane Maria," *Business Insider*, September 26, 2017, accessed June 12, 2018, http://www.businessinsider.com/trump-puerto-rico-tweet-hurricane-maria-2017-9).

53. Carlos Weber, "Isla Doncella: Puerto Rico En Crónicas by Luciérnaga Morada on Apple Podcasts," *Apple Podcasts*, October 20, 2017, accessed June 14, 2018, https://itunes.apple.com/us/podcast/isla-doncella-puerto-rico-en-cr%C3%B3nicas/id1299169441?mt=2.

54. Dickerson, "After Hurricane, Signs of a Mental Health Crisis Haunt Puerto Rico."

55. Dickerson, "After Hurricane, Signs of a Mental Health Crisis Haunt Puerto Rico."

56. Perla Rodríguez, "Piden investigar una tragedia social," *El Vocero de Puerto Rico*, November 14, 2017, accessed June 14, 2018, https://www.elvocero.com/actualidad/piden-investigar-una-tragedia-social/article_6f339ede-cc02-11e7-b9e4-bf71fa743fcc.html.

57. Casey Mendoza and James Packard, "Puerto Rico Has Cremated 911 Bodies Since Hurricane Maria," *Newsy Story*, October 28, 2017, accessed June 14, 2018, https://www.aol.com/article/news/2017/10/30/puerto-rico-has-cremated-911-bodies-since-hurricane-maria/23260681/.

58. The official number given by the government is sixty-four people. A recent study done by Harvard University estimates 4,645 deaths; see Nishant Kishore et al., "Mortality in Puerto Rico after Hurricane Maria," *New England Journal of Medicine*, May 29, 2018, accessed June 15, 2018, https://doi.org/10.1056/NEJMsa1803972.

59. Ellen Ott Marshall, *Though the Fig Tree Does Not Blossom: Toward a Responsible Theology of Christian Hope* (Nashville, TN: Abingdon Press, 2006), xvi.

60. This section is adapted from Yara González-Justiniano, "Me duele Puerto Rico" (paper presented at the American Academy of Religion Annual Meeting as part of the panel *Puerto Rico and Maria: Histories and Vulnerabilities in the Eye of the Storm*, November 2017).

61. This is where the pig curled its tail, is said when something has reached a difficult crossroad or decision.

62. Translation: "the country a sense of possibility: the feeling that things can change, that things can be changed, that people, mobilizing in the street, can change." Rafael Bernabé, Manuel Rodríguez Banchs, "Verano 19: balances y perspectivas." *80 grados*, August 2, 2019, accessed October 10, 2021, https://www.80grados.net/verano-2019-balances-y-perspectivas/

63. Charo Henríquez. Cantar, bucear, perrear y rezar: las protestas creativas en Puerto Rico. July 26, 2019, accessed October 10, 2021, https://www.nytimes.com/es/2019/07/26/espanol/america-latina/protestas-creativas-puerto-rico.html. And Simon Romero, Frances Robles, Patricia Mazzei y José A. Del Real, "Quince días de furia:

cómo se derrumbó el gobierno de Puerto Rico." July 30, 2019, accessed October 10, 2021, https://www.nytimes.com/es/2019/07/30/espanol/ricardo-rossello-renuncia-protestas.html

64. NotiCel. La carta de renuncia de Rosselló Nevares. July 25, 2019, accessed October 10, 2021, https://www.noticel.com/ahora/top-stories/20190726/la-carta-de-renuncia-de-rossello-nevares/

65. In 2014 statistics showed that about 84,000 people from the island moved to the United States. The migration of teachers and professionals is causing schools to close and interruption in services. See Jeffrey Acevedo, "Puerto Ricans Leaving Island for U.S. in Record Numbers," *CNN*, May 2, 2016, accessed August 7, 2017, http://www.cnn.com/2016/05/02/americas/puerto-rico-exodus/index.html. In the last ten years (2009–19) around 10,000 police officers have left the island in search of better pay and benefits, which has created a safety crisis. This is just one example of the ways immigration systemically affects the island and its people's future. See "Jefe del FBI reconoce que federales han fracaso en combatir el crimen en la isla," *Radio Isla 1320 AM*, January 10, 2019, accessed January 16, 2019, http://www.radioisla1320.com/jefe-del-fbi-reconoce-que-federales-han-fracaso-en-combatir-el-crimen-en-la-isla/, and "Comisionada residente entiende hay crisis de seguridad en Puerto Rico," *Radio Isla 1320 AM*, January 10, 2019, http://www.radioisla1320.com/comisionada-residente-entiende-hay-crisis-de-seguridad-en-puerto-rico/.

66. EFE, "Más de 58 mil puertorriqueños se han ido a Florida," *La Opinión* (blog), October 18, 2017, accessed October 24, 2018, https://laopinion.com/2017/10/18/mas-de-58-mil-puertorriquenos-se-han-ido-a-florida/. See also, Yarimar Bonilla, "The coloniality of disaster: Race, empire, and the temporal logics of emergency in Puerto Rico, USA," *Political Geography*, Volume 78, 2020.

67. *Lamento Borincano* is a 1929 ballad from Rafael Hernández who sings the lament of Puerto Rican farmer's economic depression.

68. See Marshall, *Though the Fig Tree Does Not Blossom*.

69. See Gustavo Gutiérrez, *The God of Life* (Maryknoll, NY: Orbis Books, 1991).

70. Miguel A. De La Torre, *Embracing Hopelessness* (Minneapolis, MN: Fortress Press, 2017).

71. De La Torre, *Embracing Hopelessness*, 5–6.

72. There is also a large immigrant community in Puerto Rico that has suffered equally or more than the native community during this period of economic depression and political instability. See "U.S. Census Bureau QuickFacts: Puerto Rico," *United States Census Bureau*, accessed November 29, 2017, https://www.census.gov/quickfacts/fact/table/pr/RHI425217#qf-headnote-a.

73. Though this expression became the motto post-hurricane, to the extent that *Coca-Cola* began printing it on its cans, it received at the same time criticism from serval Puerto Ricans who argued that the saying glossed over the dire situation of the island as it relied on optimism in a time of dire need.

74. Alves calls the systems and social orders "Organization," referring to the ways we organize society. See Rubem A. Alves, *Tomorrow's Child: Imagination, Creativity, and the Rebirth of Culture* (Eugene, OR: Wipf and Stock Publishers, 2011), 64.

75. Alves, *Tomorrow's Child*, 140.

76. Donna Borak, Rene Marsh, and Gregory Wallace, "Questions Swirl after Small Montana Firm Lands Puerto Rico Power Contract," *CNNMoney*, October 24, 2017, accessed October 25, 2017, https://money.cnn.com/2017/10/24/news/economy/puerto-rico-whitefish-trump-contract/index.html.

77. See Juan Luis Segundo, *Liberation of Theology* (Maryknoll, NY: Orbis Books, 1976).

78. I use the term "collaborator" to refer to those who contributed to my project by agreeing to be interviewed.

79. I contacted the pastor of each congregation and asked for an interview. Once on site, I participated in a church service or a community outreach event as an observer, to get an understanding of the congregation's preaching and actions. In addition to the pastors, I individually (and confidentially) interviewed two active members/lay leaders of the congregation, using a list of premeditated questions. The interviews were primarily in Spanish and, when collaborators gave permission, were recorded to assist with the accuracy of the transcription and translation.80. They took place at the church, in public locations close to the church, and in people's homes. My questions revolved around the congregation's practices and responses to the socio-economic crisis in Puerto Rico and in the aftermath of Hurricane María; their interpretation of context; and their theological responses. These interviews were transcribed and coded using a narrative analysis method, and I translated into English all passages included in the text of this book. See Catherine Kohler Riessman, *Narrative Analysis* (Newbury Park, CA: Sage Publications, 1993); Michael Quinn Patton, *Qualitative Research and Evaluation Methods* (Thousand Oaks, CA: Sage Publications, 2002); John Swinton and Harriet Mowat, *Practical Theology and Qualitative Research* (London: SCM Press, 2016).

80. According to Paulo Freire, pedagogies of solidarity ask who we are empowering in our discourse and who we are disempowering (Paulo Freire, Ana María Araújo Freire, and Walter Ferreira de Oliveira, *Pedagogy of Solidarity* [Walnut Creek, CA: Left Coast Press, 2014]).

81. The ethnographic portion of my study was open to the possibility that, in the churches I am researching, practices of hope within my categories would be limited. For example, I am searching for a holistic understanding of hope, on one hand, and practices that enact justice and flourishing through the local church's understanding of hope, on the other. It was and is possible that the churches in my sample do not understand hope or practice it within these frames. I am also aware that these practices can unfold outside of the church, or even that there might be no explicit practices. I draw my conclusions based on my observations of what *is*, not what I wanted to find. I also do not intend to develop an ultimate model but rather a model that is naturally open-ended and continuous—as seen in Juan Luis Segundo's hermeneutic circle, which provides a methodological frame of reference for my work. Although I seek to prescribe a model of liberative hope, it is essential to the hermeneutical spiral that the results are not final or closed but remain true to hope's elasticity and to the always-changing material realities of everyday life. See Marshall, *Though the Fig Tree Does Not Blossom*, 94. Discussing "lived theology," Charles Marsh writes: "Lived religion examines practices, beliefs, and objects to understand more

clearly the human phenomenon of religion, while lived theology examines practices, objects, and beliefs in order to understand God's presence in human experience." This approach puts theological analysis at the forefront of my research. For Marsh, theology is able to contribute in its own right as a field and inform other disciplines, just as other disciplines inform theology. The interviews and case studies that I did provide a glimpse of hope through lived theology, as well as a future framework for theological interpretation in my own and other disciplines. Charles Marsh et al., *Lived Theology: New Perspectives on Method, Style, and Pedagogy* (New York: Oxford University Press, 2016).

82. By using the term "Puerto Rican sayings" I do not mean the saying is of Puerto Rican origin since many of this are used in other Latin American countries.

83. *La lucha* means "the struggle." It is a popular saying coined by Latinx theologians to refer to oppressed communities' and individuals' continuous struggle for survival. See Ada María Isasi-Díaz *En La Lucha = In the Struggle: Elaborating a Mujerista Theology*, Tenth anniversary ed. Minneapolis: Fortress, 2003.

84. Alves, *Tomorrow's Child*, 199.

85. "The good people outweigh the bad."

86. González-Justiniano, "Me duele Puerto Rico," 2017.

CHAPTER TWO

1. In the aftermath of María, the mosquito population boomed. One way Puerto Ricans coped with the heat, humidity, and the excessive number of mosquito bites was through humor.

2. De La Torre, *Embracing Hopelessness*, 48–49.

3. De La Torre, *Embracing Hopelessness*, xv.

4. De La Torre, *Embracing Hopelessness*, 4–6.

5. Charity against charity is no charity. It is an expression used when a good deed is in conflict with another good deed, it turns out not being a good deed at all. Another equivalent popular expression is *"uno no desviste un santo para vestir otro"* (one does not undress a saint to dress up another saint).

6. De La Torre, *Embracing Hopelessness*, 49.

7. In the beginning of his book, De La Torre speaks about the importance of an ethics of place: to be *presente* in the spaces for which one is theologizing. He invites four scholars and one minister to be in conversation with him as he writes each of the chapters. He thus names that he is doing a less methodologically Eurocentric *"teología de* [sic] *conjunto"* (De La Torre, *Embracing Hopelessness*, xiii–xv).

8. De La Torre, *Embracing Hopelessness*, 139–40.

9. De La Torre, *Embracing Hopelessness*, 140–41.

10. Ada María Isasi-Díaz, *Mujerista Theology: A Theology for the Twenty-First Century* (Maryknoll, NY: Orbis Books, 1996), 100.

11. Isasi-Díaz, *Mujerista Theology*, 89.

12. Isasi-Díaz, *Mujerista Theology*, 101–102.

13. De La Torre, *Embracing Hopelessness*, 154.

14. De La Torre, *Embracing Hopelessness,* 149–54.

15. See Jürgen Moltmann, *Theology of Hope: On the Ground and the Implications of a Christian Eschatology* (Minneapolis, MN: Fortress Press, 1993).

16. As well as other scholars like De La Torre and Moltmann, Dermot Lane occasionally argues for Christian hope interchangeably with the understandings of eschatology (see *Keeping Hope Alive: Stirrings in Christian Theology* [New York: Paulist Press, 1996], 2).

17. Dominic Doyle, "A Future, Difficult, Yet Possible Good: Defining Christian Hope," in *Hope: Promise, Possibility and Fulfillment,* eds. Richard Lennan and Nancy Pineda-Madrid (New York: Paulist Press, 2013), 24.

18. Doyle, "A Future, Difficult, Yet Possible Good," 24. See Moltmann, *Theology of Hope,* 93–95.

19. De La Torre, *Embracing Hopelessness,* 139–40.

20. Colleen M. Griffith, "Christian Hope: A Grace and a Choice," in *Hope: Promise, Possibility and Fulfillment,* eds. Nancy Pineda Madrid, and Richard Lennan (New York: Paulist Press, 2013), 6.

21. Where there is life, there is hope. In the text I use the Spanish bible translation *Palabra de Dios Para Todos.* See Elsa Támez, *Bajo un Cielo Sin Estrellas: Lecturas y Meditaciones Bíblicas* (Costa Rica: Editorial Departamento Ecuménico de Investigación, 2004), 75. Life is understood in a broad sense, not just a the material presence of life but also refers to life abundant.

22. Lauren Gail Berlant, *Cruel Optimism* (Durham, NC: Duke University Press, 2011), 1. Walter Earl Fluker would call this "perverted hope" (*The Ground Has Shifted: The Future of the Black Church in Post-Racial America* [New York: New York University Press, 2016], 39).

23. Berlant, *Cruel Optimism,* 14.

24. Emily Dianne Cram, review of *Cruel Optimism* by Lauren Berlant, *Rhetoric & Public Affairs* 17, no. 2 (June 23, 2014): 371–74.

25. Ellen Ott Marshall and Orlando Espín argue that hope is not optimism because it trivializes suffering. See Marshall, *Though the Fig Tree Does Not Blossom,* 2; Orlando Espín, *Idol and Grace: On Traditioning and Subversive Hope* (Maryknoll, NY: Orbis Books, 2014).

26. Rubem Alves talks about magic as those rationally 'impossible' beliefs people hold on to. He uses the example of dancing for rain. "Magic is imagination taking hold of the body; imagination is the secret form of magic" (*Tomorrow's Child,* 73–84).

27. Rafael Bernabe, "Manifiesto de la esperanza sin optimismo en Puerto Rico," *80grados* (blog), November 24, 2017, accessed October 30, 2018, http://www.80grados.net/manifiesto-de-la-esperanza-sin-optimismo-en-puerto-rico/.

28. "Optimism doesn't give us much to go off from, true, but hope can be nurtured by pessimism . . . we have to search and we have to hold on to any possibility of change" (Bernabe, "Manifiesto de la esperanza sin optimismo en Puerto Rico").

29. Yarimar Bonilla, *Non-Sovereign Futures: French Caribbean Politics in the Wake of Disenchantment* (Chicago: The University of Chicago Press, 2015), 172.

30. Alves, *Tomorrow's Child,* 111.

31. The creative act is what Alves believes will open ourselves to a different future where humans are guided by their desires and we make do with the logic of the dinosaur (*Tomorrow's Child*, 36). Jürgen Moltmann talks about creative action as the catalyst partner of hope and salvation with the weaving of history and reality. A creative act that springs from a faith that comes from hope for it shows an anticipation of possibilities and prospects (*Theology of Hope*, 35).

32. Alves, *Tomorrow's Child*, 142–44.
33. Alves, *Tomorrow's Child*, 151.
34. Alves, *Tomorrow's Child*, 152.
35. Alves, *Tomorrow's Child*, 153–54.
36. Monica A. Coleman, *Making a Way Out of No Way: A Womanist Theology* (Minneapolis, MN: Fortress Press, 2008), 85.
37. Coleman, *Making a Way Out of No Way*, 85–86.
38. See Steven Michael Rodenborn, *Hope in Action: Subversive Eschatology in the Theology of Edward Schillebeeckx and Johann Baptist Metz* (Minneapolis, MN: Fortress Press, 2014).
39. Moltmann, *Theology of Hope*, 13.
40. Moltmann, *Theology of Hope*, 16.
41. Moltmann, *Theology of Hope*, 16.
42. Ernst Bloch, *The Principle of Hope* (Cambridge, MA: MIT Press, 1986), 1375.
43. Moltmann, *Theology of Hope*, 17.
44. Moltmann, *Theology of Hope*, 30.
45. Moltmann, *Theology of Hope*, 20.
46. Moltmann, *Theology of Hope*, 168.
47. Moltmann, *Theology of Hope*, 34.
48. Jürgen Moltmann, *Hope and Planning* (New York: Harper & Row, 1971), 178.
49. Jürgen Moltmann, *The Living God and the Fullness of Life* (Louisville, KY: Westminster John Knox Press, 2015), 189.
50. Moltmann, *Theology of Hope*, 319.
51. Moltmann, *Theology of Hope*, 32.
52. Moltmann, *Theology of Hope*, 315.
53. Marshall, *Though the Fig Tree Does Not Blossom*, xiii–xiv.
54. Marshall, *Though the Fig Tree Does Not Blossom*, xvi, 78.
55. Coleman understands that relationships are not limited to humans with other humans but humans with nature and God's justice extends to them (*Making a Way Out of No Way*, 85–94).
56. Marshall, *Though the Fig Tree Does Not Blossom*, xiv.
57. Marshall, *Though the Fig Tree Does Not Blossom*, 94.
58. Marshall, *Though the Fig Tree Does Not Blossom*, 107.
59. See Gerardo E. Alvarado León, "El Gobierno Mercadea 17 Terrenos Protegidos," *El Nuevo Día*, accessed September 19, 2018, https://www.elnuevodia.com/noticias/locales/nota/elgobiernomercadea17terrenosprotegidos-2421335/.
60. Personal conversation, November, 2017.
61. Marshall, *Though the Fig Tree Does Not Blossom*, 107.
62. Moltmann, *Theology of Hope*, 18.

63. Kin-dom is a term coined by Ada María Isasi-Díaz to avoid a presumption of the dominion of God being male. "The word kin-dom makes it clear that when the fullness of God becomes a day-to-day reality in the world at large . . . we will all be kin to each other" (Ada Maria Isasi-Diaz, *En La Lucha/In the Struggle: Elaborating a Mujerista Theology* [Minneapolis, MN: Fortress Press, 2004], 213).

64. Alves uses the word Organization, stemming from the word organ, as the task of transforming and grouping things that are unrelated, not functional or unrelated into a functional thing. It is the way (means) we systematize our world in order for it to make 'sense' (Alves, *Tomorrow's Child*, 15).

65. Alves, *Tomorrow's Child*, 63.

66. Alves, *Tomorrow's Child*, 2.

67. Any alignment with our historical present is not just a coincidence; Alves wrote this book in the first half of the 1970s while at Union Theological Seminary in New York City (*Tomorrow's Child*, 2).

68. Alves, *Tomorrow's Child*, 2.

69. Alves, *Tomorrow's Child*, 3.

70. Alves, *Tomorrow's Child*, 5.

71. Alves, *Tomorrow's Child*, 6.

72. The author heavily critiques the use of science for military purposes, noting that since science is at the mercy of economic powers and not for the purpose of human creativity, it helps power succeed in its future (*Tomorrow's Child*, 10–11, 25).

73. Alves, *Tomorrow's Child*, 11–13.

74. Alves, *Tomorrow's Child*, 16–17.

75. Alves, *Tomorrow's Child*, 89.

76. Alves, *Tomorrow's Child*, 24.

77. This act of moving from product to product is only afforded to those with the power to acquire it, which makes one wonder about how Alves understands and categorizes his social theories to class and economic solvency (Alves, *Tomorrow's Child*, 26–33).

78. Alves, *Tomorrow's Child*, 34–35.

79. Alves, *Tomorrow's Child*, 31.

80. Alves, *Tomorrow's Child*, 55.

81. Alves, *Tomorrow's Child*, 63–66.

82. Alves, *Tomorrow's Child*, 91–95.

83. Alves, *Tomorrow's Child*, 106.

84. Alves, *Tomorrow's Child*, 103, 199, 201.

85. Alves, *Tomorrow's Child*, 111–12.

86. Alves, *Tomorrow's Child*, 114.

87. Alves, *Tomorrow's Child*, 197.

88. Alves, *Tomorrow's Child*, 115.

89. Alves, *Tomorrow's Child*, 173.

90. Alves, *Tomorrow's Child*, 194.

91. Alves, *Tomorrow's Child*, 196–97.

92. Alves, *Tomorrow's Child*, 204.

93. John D. Caputo, *Hoping Against Hope: Confessions of a Postmodern Pilgrim* (Minneapolis, MN: Fortress Press, 2015), 198–99.
94. Sergio Arce Martínez, *¿Cómo Es Que Aún No Entendéis?: Antología de Textos Teológicos*, vol. 1 (La Habana, Cuba: Editorial Caminos, 2009).
95. Lane, *Keeping Hope Alive*, 2.
96. Gloria Anzaldúa, *Borderlands/La Frontera: The New Mestiza* (San Francisco: Aunt Lute Books, 2007), 60.
97. Faculties.
98. See Aristotle, *Categories*, trans. E. M. Edghill (Blacksburg, VA: Virginia Tech, 2001).
99. Caputo, *Hoping Against Hope*, 199.
100. Griffith, "Christian Hope: A Grace and a Choice," 9.
101. Griffith, "Christian Hope: A Grace and a Choice," 13.
102. Marshall, *Though the Fig Tree Does Not Blossom*, xiii–xiv.
103. Nancy Pineda-Madrid, "Hope and Salvation in the Shadow of Tragedy," in *Hope: Promise, Possibility and Fulfillment*, eds. Nancy Pineda Madrid, and Richard Lennan (New York: Paulist Press, 2013), 125.
104. Alves, *Tomorrow's Child*, 80.
105. Jürgen Moltmann, *The Church in the Power of the Spirit: A Contribution to Messianic Ecclesiology* (Minneapolis, MN: Fortress Press, 1993), 75.
106. Protestant ministers, traditionally, were United Statesians. After the great depression they started immigrating back to the States; therefore, the pastoring of the churches relayed on local leaders. See Krenly Cruz, *Historia Del Avivamiento Del '33 de Los Discípulos de Cristo En Puerto Rico* (Bogotá, Colombia: Editorial Buena Semilla, 2003).
107. Lane, *Keeping Hope Alive*, 57.
108. Caputo, *Hoping Against Hope*, 199.

CHAPTER THREE

1. Alves, *Tomorrow's Child*, 171.
2. Melissa Pagán, "PUERTO RICO FORUM REFLECTION #3: Cultivating a Hermeneutics of 'El Grito' in the Eye of the Storm," *Perspectivas Online*, accessed November 5, 2018, http://perspectivasonline.com/downloads/cultivating-a-hermeneutics-of-el-grito-in-the-eye-of-the-storm/.
3. Rodenborn, *Hope in Action*, 290.
4. Gloria Anzaldúa, *Light in the Dark = Luz En Lo Oscuro: Rewriting Identity, Spirituality, Reality* (Durham, NC: Duke University Press, 2015), 21.
5. "Iglesias Cristianas en Puerto Rico," *Puerto Rico Government Open Data Portal*, accessed December 7, 2018, https://data.pr.gov/Negocios-y-Corporaciones-/Iglesias-Cristianas-en-Puerto-Rico/b6tz-fhap. This number might be higher since denominations register as a whole and do not register individual local congregations.
6. See Gloria Ruiz Kuilan, "Ricardo Rosselló puso sobre la mesa reforma laboral modificada," *El Nuevo Día*, March 22, 2018, accessed January 7, 2019, https://www

.elnuevodia.com/noticias/politica/nota/ricardorossellopusosobrelamesareformalaboralmodificada-2408458/.

7. Not all collaborators agreed to voice recording; when they requested, I took notes instead.

8. Based on stories I have gathered from friends and pastor colleagues on the island, special attention needs to be given to the youth's experience of María and the island's economic depression. I would think the same should apply to a reading of hope through their experience. See Mary Elizabeth Moore and Yara González-Justiniano, "Youth Wisdom: Pointing Toward Joy and Flourishing," January 10, 2018), https://www.youtube.com/watch?v=VG431sR2aFE, and Evelyn L. Parker, *Trouble Don't Last Always: Emancipatory Hope Among African American Adolescents* (Cleveland, OH: Pilgrim Press, 2003), 9.

9. In *Ecos del Seminario,* Puerto Rico's Evangelical Seminary's journal, Rev. Dr. Agustina Luvis Nuñez recounts an encounter with an older woman in her residential community who, ever since she could remember, had been homeless. When Dr. Luvis asked her how she was doing post-María, the older woman responded "well"; she had nothing, so María couldn't take anything away from her. One of the things María revealed to the unseeing eye was the rampant poverty many people had long lived with on the island. Certainly, my sample privileges one sector of the population. People living in extreme poverty, or even rich people's, experiences vary from what I present here. For example, people who in hindsight describe the Hurricane as a blessing because of the lessons learned may differ from those who lost everything. See Agustina Luvis Nuñez, "Pa' atrás, ni pá tomar impulso," *Ecos del Seminario* 2 (2018): 5–6, accessed December 24, 2018, (available at https://www.calameo.com/read/00138258213253d9aa28b).

10. Their surprise around ecumenism and their lack of explicitness in acknowledging non-Christian churches in the island leads me to assume that interreligious dialogue, although it exists in very small circles like the *Colectivo Interreligioso de Mujeres* (Women's Interreligious Collective) and *Mesa de Diálogo Martin Luther King Jr.*, is not a priority or an acknowledged need. Collaborator #16 said that *"Puerto Rico es un país Cristiano"* (Puerto Rico is a Christian country). I lack statistics, because these populations are made invisible, but there are *santeros(as),* Jewish and Muslim, and Hare Krishna practitioners, to name a few. This also speaks to the privilege Christianity has in the public and political sphere in the island. See Collaborator #16, confidential interview by Yara González-Justiniano, Puerto Rico, March-April, 2018; this and subsequent translations from all collaborators except #6 and #7 (who were interviewed in English) are by Yara González-Justiniano.

11. *Mar Azul* has an extensive list of ministries and outreach programs. As with the rest of the congregations, most involved in countless ministries, I limit myself to mentioning one or two.

12. Collaborator #9, confidential interview by Yara González-Justiniano, Puerto Rico, March-April, 2018.

13. See José Enrique Laboy Goméz, "Entre Sotanas y Desobediencia Civil: De Antulio Parrilla a 'Felo' Torres," *Claridad*, accessed August 24, 2018, http://www

.claridadpuertorico.com/content.html?news=6242FD91DBDB7AC90B844AB92C5E1E39.

14. Impuesto sobre Ventas y Usos (Sale and Use Tax) was the 7% taxation implemented in 2006. In 2016 this was changed to an 11.5% I.V.A (Value Added Tax). See Ricardo Cortés Chico, "The Change from IVU to IVA," *El Nuevo Día*, February 18, 2015, accessed August 24, 2018, http://www.elnuevodia.com/negocios/consumo/nota/thechangefromivutoiva-2011618/.

15. See "Iglesias se unen por excarcelación de Oscar López," *El Nuevo Día*, September 19, 2014, accessed August 17, 2018, http://www.elnuevodia.com/noticias/locales/nota/iglesiasseunenporexcarcelaciondeoscarlopez-1858131/; United Methodist Communications, "¿Por qué las iglesias metodistas apoyaron la liberación de López Rivera?," *Portal en español*, accessed August 14, 2018, http://hispanic.umc.org/news/porque-las-iglesias-metodistas-apoyaron-la-liberacion-de-lopez-rivera.

16. "May the crucifixion of our people not be indifferent to us." *Todos Somos Pueblo* is a collective of community organizers led by Father Pedro Ortíz. See "Califican de Pecado Las 'agresiones Del Estado,'" *Primera Hora*, March 29, 2018, accessed August, 2018, http://www.primerahora.com/noticias/gobierno-politica/nota/calificandepecadolasagresionesdelestado-1275120/.

17. "Protest" is going to a march against the rise of gasoline costs; an act of resistance would be to not buy the gasoline (Alves, *Tomorrow's Child*, 22–23).

18. Alberto Melucci, *Challenging Codes: Collective Action in the Information Age* (Cambridge: Cambridge University Press, 1996), 4.

19. Melucci, *Challenging Codes*, 6–7.

20. Melucci, *Challenging Codes*, 10.

21. Melucci, *Challenging Codes*, 53.

22. Melucci, *Challenging Codes*, 290–95.

23. Gervasio L. García, *Desafío y Solidaridad: Breve Historia Del Movimiento Obrero Puertorriqueño* (Río Piedras, PR: Ediciones Huracán, 1997), 18.

24. García, *Desafío y Solidaridad*, 69.

25. García, *Desafío y Solidaridad*, 18.

26. García, *Desafío y Solidaridad*, 32.

27. García, *Desafío y Solidaridad*, 134–35. Walter Earl Fluker also speaks of the other side of education racial uplift: its perpetuation of difference and separation (*The Ground Has Shifted*, 36).

28. Many of these movements have struggled to enact systemic change because (unlike the Workers' Movement with its class-struggle analysis that sought to change the underlying organization of work and economic relationships) they are not strongly equipped to address the intersectional challenges that created the issues in the first place.

29. See Keila López Alicea, "Derogan carta circular de Educación sobre equidad de género," *El Nuevo Día*, February 8, 2017, accessed August 24, 2018, http://www.elnuevodia.com/noticias/locales/nota/derogancartacirculardeeducacionsobreequidaddegenero-2289384/; César Vázquez Muñiz, "PR por la Familia rechaza proyectos del Senado que atentan contra nuestros niños," *Puerto Rico por la Familia* (blog), August 16, 2013, accessed August 24, 2018, https://prporlafamilia.com/

comunicados-de-prensa/pr-por-la-familia-rechaza-proyectos-del-senado-que-atentan-contra-nuestros-ninos/.

30. Alejandro Cotté Morales et al., *Trabajo Comunitario y Descolonización* (San Juan, PR: Fundación Francisco Manrique Cabrera, 2012), 36.

31. Cotté Morales et al., *Trabajo Comunitario y Descolonización*, 203–7.

32. Cotté Morales et al., *Trabajo Comunitario y Descolonización*, 36.

33. Melucci, *Challenging Codes*, 295. See also Saul Alinsky, *Rules for Radicals: A Practical Primer for Realistic Radicals* (New York: Random House, 1971).

34. Cotté Morales et al., *Trabajo Comunitario y Descolonización*, 237–41.

35. Alinsky, *Rules for Radicals*, 56.

36. "The church is not always going be the lead singer," an expression used to say that the subject is not always the center of attention.

37. Anzaldúa, *Borderlands/La Frontera*, 65.

38. Roberto Velez, "'Because History Does Not Allow Us . . .': Collective Memory and the Articulation of Mobilization Narratives in the Antimilitary Movement of Vieques (1999–2003)" (PhD diss., University of Albany, 2018), 207.

39. Velez, "Because History Does Not Allow Us . . . ," 217.

40. Gutiérrez, *A Theology of Liberation*, 147.

41. See Jon Sobrino, "The Economics of the Poor," in *The True Church and the Poor* (Maryknoll, NY: Orbis Books, 1984), and Cláudio Carvalhaes, "Hasta Que Salga El Sol" (paper presented at Theopoetics: A Transdisciplinary Conference, Boston University School of Theology, 2016).

42. Leonardo Boff, *Ecclesiogenesis: The Base Communities Reinvent the Church* (Maryknoll, NY: Orbis Books, 1986), 49.

43. Gutiérrez, *The God of Life*, xii.

44. Letty M. Russell, *Church in the Round: Feminist Interpretation of the Church* (Louisville, KY: Westminster John Knox Press, 1993), 113.

45. Jung Young Lee, *Marginality: The Key to Multicultural Theology* (Minneapolis, MN: Fortress Press, 1995), 101.

46. Lee, *Marginality*, 121–22.

47. Boff, *Ecclesiogenesis*, 5.

48. Gutiérrez, *A Theology of Liberation*, 287.

49. Lee, *Marginality*, 121–22.

50. Roberto S. Goizueta, "Corpus Verum: Toward a Borderland Ecclesiology," in *Building Bridges, Doing Justice: Constructing a Latino/a Ecumenical Theology*, ed. Orlando O. Espín (Maryknoll, NY: Orbis Books, 2009), 147.

51. The quotation is from the benediction liturgy at Pub Church, Boston, MA.

52. Russell, *Church in the Round*, 145.

53. Boff, *Ecclesiogenesis*, 53.

54. John Fife, "Sanctuary Movement" (paper presented at the Wilderness Theology and the U.S. Mexico Border Travel Seminar, Tucson, AZ, January 7, 2016).

55. Jon Sobrino, "The Economics of Ecclesia: A Poor Church Is a Church Rich in Compassion," in *New Visions for the Americas: Religious Engagement and Social Transformation* (Minneapolis, MN: Fortress Press, 1993), 83–84.

56. Sobrino, "The Economics of Ecclesia," 87–89.

57. Russell, *Church in the Round*, 121–22.
58. Elizabeth Conde-Frazier, "Being the Gospel Together: The Marks of an Evangélica Ecclesiology," in *Latina Evangélicas: A Theological Survey from the Margins*, eds. Loida Martell-Otero, Zaida Maldonado Pérez, and Elizabeth Conde-Frazier (Eugene, OR: Cascade Books, 2013), 101–2.
59. See Boff, *Ecclesiogenesis*, 24, and Moltmann, *The Church in the Power of the Spirit*.
60. Gutiérrez, *A Theology of Liberation*, 170.
61. "Make hearts out of intestines," an expression used to signify that you make what you need with what you have.
62. "Neither our hope nor security is not in anything material. Everything fell" (Collaborator #18, confidential interview by Yara González-Justiniano, Puerto Rico, March-April 2018).
63. "*Aquí todos los días nos quitan la esperanza.*" "Here, our hope is taken away every day." (Collaborator #18, confidential interview by Yara González-Justiniano, Puerto Rico, March-April 2018).
64. "Tribulation is an aspect of knowing what we hope for" (Collaborator #12, confidential interview by Yara González-Justiniano, Puerto Rico, March-April 2018.) Collaborator #12 also mentioned the importance of lament in our path of hope and a mature faith; we need to truly examine our mistakes as a society and as a church so our faith does not become a caricature.
65. "Hope needs to keep us joyful" (Collaborator #12, confidential interview by Yara González-Justiniano, Puerto Rico, March-April 2018).
66. Collaborators #1, 13, 14, 17, 8, and 19, confidential interviews by Yara González-Justiniano, Puerto Rico, March-April, 2018.
67. Collaborators #13, 15, and 18, confidential interviews by Yara González-Justiniano, Puerto Rico, March-April, 2018.
68. Collaborators #1, 7, 13, 14, and 16, confidential interviews by Yara González-Justiniano, Puerto Rico, March-April, 2018.
69. "Hope transcends what we own, hope transcends what we see. It is that hook we hold on to so we can cross the river of hardship. Without hope we die. I think what hope does is make us desire life, desire a tomorrow. It is what makes us move in opposite directions to what our will would be" (Collaborator #8, confidential interview by Yara González-Justiniano, Puerto Rico, March-April, 2018).
70. "Hope with faith can make us more sensitive and love more. It is like a dream. It is centered in Christ" (Collaborator #17, confidential interview by Yara González-Justiniano, Puerto Rico, March-April, 2018. Collaborator #12 also referred to hope as a dream.
71. Collaborator #1, 18, and 19, confidential interviews by Yara González-Justiniano, Puerto Rico, March-April, 2018.
72. Collaborators #1, 2, 4, 14, 15, 16, and 18, confidential interviews by Yara González-Justiniano, Puerto Rico, March-April, 2018.
73. Collaborators #3, 4, and 16, confidential interviews by Yara González-Justiniano, Puerto Rico, March-April, 2018.

74. Collaborators #1 and 13, confidential interviews by Yara González-Justiniano, Puerto Rico, March-April, 2018.

75. Collaborators #3, 4, 5, 7, 13, 16, and 18, confidential interviews by Yara González-Justiniano, Puerto Rico, March-April, 2018.

76. "What, in these situations of tribulation, helps us contemplate another reality in God" (Collaborator #1, confidential interviews by Yara González-Justiniano, Puerto Rico, March-April, 2018).

77. "Hope is in the fact that we are being trained" (Collaborator #16, confidential interview by Yara González-Justiniano, Puerto Rico, March-April, 2018).

78. Collaborator #7, confidential interview by Yara González-Justiniano, Puerto Rico, March-April, 2018.

79. "Hope is the virtue of waiting in God's promises, for the wellbeing of God's people will always be fulfilled" (Collaborator #9, confidential interview by Yara González-Justiniano, Puerto Rico, March-April, 2018).

80. Collaborators #1, 9, 13, 17, 18, and 19, confidential interviews by Yara González-Justiniano, Puerto Rico, March-April, 2018.

81. Collaborators #4, 5, and 15, confidential interviews by Yara González-Justiniano, Puerto Rico, March-April, 2018.

82. "It is here where one starts having an experience with people where one is a blessing and a believable alternative of God's power" (Collaborator #1, confidential interview by Yara González-Justiniano, Puerto Rico, March-April, 2018).

83. "Hope, before it can be communal, it has to be born from inside you. I live my hope with my example. You cannot fake hope for a long time. Hope is birthed inside of you and then it overflows" (Collaborator #4, confidential interview by Yara González-Justiniano, Puerto Rico, March-April, 2018).

84. Collaborators #14 and 16, confidential interviews by Yara González-Justiniano, Puerto Rico, March-April, 2018.

85. Collaborator #18, confidential interview by Yara González-Justiniano, Puerto Rico, March-April, 2018.

86. Collaborator #4 spoke of material change as not only about physical structures; they also referred to education, provision of work, and communitarian development incorporating economic, social, spiritual and emotional change (confidential interview by Yara González-Justiniano, Puerto Rico, March-April, 2018).

87. Collaborators #2, 4, 12 and 17, confidential interviews by Yara González-Justiniano, Puerto Rico, March-April, 2018.

88. Collaborator #4, confidential interview by Yara González-Justiniano, Puerto Rico, March-April, 2018.

89. Collaborators #2, 13, and 17, confidential interviews by Yara González-Justiniano, Puerto Rico, March-April, 2018.

90. "Jesus came to decolonize" (Collaborator #14, confidential interview by Yara González-Justiniano, Puerto Rico, March-April, 2018).

91. Collaborators #5, 7, and 12, confidential interview by Yara González-Justiniano, Puerto Rico, March-April, 2018.

92. Collaborator #17, confidential interview by Yara González-Justiniano, Puerto Rico, March-April, 2018.

93. "The best theology is the one you live out" (Collaborator #4, confidential interview by Yara González-Justiniano, Puerto Rico, March-April, 2018).
94. Collaborators #3, 4, 5, 10, 16, and 18, confidential interview by Yara González-Justiniano, Puerto Rico, March-April, 2018.
95. Collaborators #1, 3, and 12, confidential interview by Yara González-Justiniano, Puerto Rico, March-April, 2018.
96. Collaborator #1, confidential interview by Yara González-Justiniano, Puerto Rico, March-April, 2018.
97. "Definitely, the church was one of those arteries where the blood of hope circulated to get to the families" (Collaborator #12, confidential interviews by Yara González-Justiniano, Puerto Rico, March-April, 2018).

CHAPTER FOUR

1. See Paul Ricœur, *Memory, History, Forgetting* (Chicago: University of Chicago Press, 2004).
2. See Fluker, *The Ground Has Shifted*; Joseph Richard Winters, *Hope Draped in Black: Race, Melancholy, and the Agony of Progress* (Durham, NC: Duke University Press, 2016); and Gustavo Gutiérrez, *The Power of the Poor in History: Selected Writings* (Maryknoll, NY: Orbis Books, 1983).
3. Walter Benjamin, "The Storyteller and 'Theses on the Philosophy of History,'" in *The Collective Memory Reader*, eds. Jeffrey K. Olick, Vered Vinitzky-Seroussi, and David Levy (New York: Oxford University Press, 2011), 99–103.
4. Milan Kundera, *The Book of Laughter and Forgetting* (New York: Harper Perennial Modern Classics, 1999), 4.
5. Benjamin, "The Storyteller," 102.
6. Dori Laub, "An Event Without a Witness: Truth, Testimony," in *Testimony: Crises of Witnessing in Literature, Psychoanalysis and History* (New York: Routledge, 1992), 83, and Dori Laub, "Bearing Witness, or the Vicissitudes of Listening," in *Testimony*, 71.
7. Chris Weedon and Glenn Jordan, "Collective Memory: Theory and Politics," *Social Semiotics* 22, no. 2 (2012): 143.
8. Maurice Halbwachs, *On Collective Memory*, ed. Lewis A. Coser (Chicago: University of Chicago Press, 1992), 51.
9. Weedon and Jordan, "Collective Memory," 150.
10. Collective Memory studies are quite broad. My approach to the topic is mainly sociological and anthropological; other veins of memory studies focus on history and psychology.
11. Halbwachs, *On Collective Memory*, 17.
12. Halbwachs, *On Collective Memory*, 184.
13. Jeffrey K. Olick, Vered Vinitzky-Seroussi, and Daniel Levy, eds., *The Collective Memory Reader* (New York: Oxford University Press, 2011), 18.
14. Pierre Nora, "Between Memory and History: Les Lieux de Mémoire," *Representations* 26, no. 26 (1989): 12.

15. Nora, "Between Memory and History," 14.
16. Nora, "Between Memory and History," 11.
17. A *milieu de mémoire* is an actual environment of memory where memory is part of everyday experience (Pierre Nora, *Realms of Memory: Rethinking the French Past*, vol. 1 [New York: Columbia University Press, 1996], 1).
18. I am not saying the Church is a site of memory in its fullness, but it can be a site of memory. Some churches become petrified in time in a society that has banished ritual and Christianity; note how many church buildings are being repurposed.
19. Nora, *Realms of Memory*, 6–9.
20. See Nora, *Realms of Memory*, 4.
21. He is not just referring to rituals, but to habitus (Paul Connerton, *How Societies Remember* [Cambridge: Cambridge University Press, 1989], 91).
22. Connerton, *How Societies Remember*, 38.
23. Nora, *Realms of Memory*, 4.
24. Ricardo Roselló, the island's governor at the time, signed a law that took the day of the Puerto Rican constitution out of the holidays list and made a new holiday celebrating American citizenship. See Rebecca Banuchi, "El gobierno eliminará el feriado del 25 de julio," *El Nuevo Día*, April 28, 2017, accessed December 20, 2018, https://www.elnuevodia.com/noticias/politica/nota/elgobiernoeliminaraelferiadodel2 5dejulio-2315552/.
25. Written by Manuel Fernández Juncos in 1903, Puerto Rico's national anthem speaks about Christopher Columbus's admiration of the island's beauty. It substituted the anthem written in 1868 by poet Lola Rodríguez de Tió, sung as a call of revolution, and was deemed seditious after the United States' invasion.
26. Ron Eyerman, "From the Past in the Present: Culture and the Transmission of Memory," in *The Collective Memory Reader*, 305.
27. Yael Zerubavel, "From Recovered Roots: Collective Memory and the Making of Israeli National Tradition," in *The Collective Memory Reader*, 237.
28. Zerubavel, "From Recovered Roots," 237–38.
29. Zerubavel, "From Recovered Roots," 239.
30. Zerubavel, "From Recovered Roots," 241.
31. Connerton, *How Societies Remember*, 36.
32. Jorge Mendoza García, "Exordio a La Memoria Colectiva y El Olvido Social," *Athenea Digital* 8 (2005), 10–11.
33. Mendoza García, "Exordio a La Memoria Colectiva y El Olvido Social," 32.
34. Mendoza García, "Exordio a La Memoria Colectiva y El Olvido Social," 17–18.
35. Mendoza García, "Exordio a La Memoria Colectiva y El Olvido Social," 17–18.
36. Bradford Vivian, *Public Forgetting: The Rhetoric and Politics of Beginning Again* (University Park, PA: Pennsylvania State University, 2010), 124.
37. Vivian, *Public Forgetting,* 181.
38. Isasi-Díaz, *Mujerista Theology*, 15.
39. Halbwachs, *On Collective Memory*, 51.
40. Delgado, *A Puerto Rican Decolonial Theology,* 14.

41. "Since it is not Latin American or North American it ends up erased. Many do not see a historical subject, nor aim. Puerto Rican history is a tale that does not matter, and therefore, it is not told. It is not before or after, it is outside, without complexity, without internal heterogeneity, without affective or political tensions. It is pure nonbeing. Exclusion has been the norm. That which is Puerto Rican is an eternal forgotten and despised frontier, or a neutral untrusted space. Dominating national and cultural categories in the United States and Latin America, and the Puerto Rican colonial situation, frequently move towards the negation of historical memory, or to place it in a disdainful or paternalistic 'outside,' almost always enigmatic. It is a memory at many times negated, and broken" (Arcadio Díaz Quiñones, *La Memoria Rota* [San Juan, PR: Ediciones Huracán, 1996], 79, italic emphasis and translation mine).

42. Coloniality of power is a concept explored further by Anibal Quijano that focuses on the connection the practices and history of colonialism embedded in social systems and ways of knowing. See Walter Mignolo, *Local Histories/Global Designs: Coloniality, Subaltern Knowledges, and Border Thinking* (Princeton, NJ: Princeton University Press, 2000).

43. Anzaldúa, *Light in the Dark = Luz En Lo Oscuro*, 19–20.

44. Anzaldúa, *Light in the Dark = Luz En Lo Oscuro*, 21.

45. See Paul Connerton, *The Spirit of Mourning: History, Memory and the Body* (Cambridge: Cambridge University Press, 2011).

46. See Johann Baptist Metz, *Faith in History and Society: Toward a Practical Fundamental Theology* (New York: Seabury Press, 1980).

47. Fluker, *The Ground Has Shifted*, 39.

48. Fluker, *The Ground Has Shifted*, 39.

49. Velez, "'Because History Does Not Allow Us . . . ,'" 207, 211.

50. Fluker, *The Ground Has Shifted*, 40.

51. Vélez, "'Because History Does Not Allow Us . . . ,'" 217.

52. "From utterance to action, there is a long road."

53. Alves, *A Theology of Human Hope*, 24. See also Filipe Maia, "Toward a Theology of Liberation (Again)" (paper presented at the American Academy of Religion Annual Meeting, Denver, Colorado, November 2018, on the panel *Extra, Extra! The End Is Here: Apocalypsis 2018*).

54. Rubem A. Alves, *The Poet, the Warrior, the Prophet: The Edward Cadbury Lectures 1990*, (London: SCM, 2002).

55. Anzaldúa, *Light in the Dark = Luz En Lo Oscuro*, 20–21.

56. Chapter 2 discusses Sergio Arce's work and Johann Baptist Metz's emphasis on the creation narrative over the exodus narrative in the Scriptures.

57. I use the word "bodies" rather than "humans" because I want to include other living creatures and bodies of nature in this understanding of liberation.

58. Gutiérrez, *A Theology of Liberation*, 87.

59. Sebastián Robiou Lamarche, *Mitología y Religión de Los Taínos* (San Juan, PR: Editorial Punto y Coma, 2006), 17.

60. Sergio Arce Martínez, *Teología En Revolución*, vol. 1 (Matanzas, Cuba: Centro de Información y Estudio Augusto Cotto, 1975), 35–36.

61. "Any reconstruction of nation (a people) fundamentally means to end the fragmentation of the human being" (Arce Martínez, ¿Cómo Es Que Aún No Entendéis?, 98, translation mine).

62. Arce Martínez, *Teología En Revolución*, 2–3.

63. Alves, *A Theology of Human Hope*, 23.

64. Alves, *A Theology of Human Hope*, 28.

65. Alves, *A Theology of Human Hope*, 28–34.

66. "FEMA Mudará a los Damnificados del Huracán María a los Estados Unidos," *El Nuevo Día*, November 9, 2017, accessed December 28, 2018, https://www.elnuevodia.com/noticias/locales/nota/femamudaraalosdamnificadosdelhuracanmariaalosestadosunidos-2372913/.

67. George E. Tinker, *Spirit and Resistance: Political Theology and American Indian Liberation* (Minneapolis, MN: Fortress Press, 2004), 111.

68. Tinker, *Spirit and Resistance*, 100.

69. Tinker, *Spirit and Resistance*, 101.

70. Tinker, *Spirit and Resistance*, 111–12. See also Jeanette Rodriguez, "La Tierra Theologies' Contributions to Creation Theologies," in *In Our Own Voices: Latino/a Renditions of Theology*, ed. Benjamín Valentín (Maryknoll, NY: Orbis Books, 2010), 21–40.

71. Mayra Mayra, *Poetics of the Flesh*, (Durham, NC: Duke University Press, 2015), 145.

72. Teresa Delgado, "Freedom Is Our Own: Towards a Puerto Rican Emancipation Theology," in *Creating Ourselves: African Americans and Hispanic Americans on Popular Culture and Religious Expression*, ed. Anthony Pinn and Benjamín Valentín (Durham, NC: Duke University Press, 2009), 145.

73. Judith Butler, Zeynep Gambetti, and Leticia Sabsay, *Vulnerability in Resistance* (Durham, NC: Duke University Press, 2016), 1.

74. Gutiérrez makes an analysis from the economical basis that shapes the identity of a country as developed or underdeveloped and tries to move away from this language. Regardless of his understanding of the word "development" as signifying process and well-being, he opts for the use of the word liberation. This is so especially because the term development was first employed to describe the process an undeveloped country went through when bought by a rich country, and underdevelopment is a result of the development of other countries. The author seeks a theology that encloses a "liberation of everything that limits or impedes man's realization of himself, of all of that which impedes the access—or exercise of—their freedom" (*A Theology of Liberation*, 74–79, 80).

75. Yara González-Justiniano, "Resistencia en Conjunto: A Practice in Radical Solidarity and the Embodiment of the Eucharist" (paper presented at the conference *Beyond the Margins: Indecent Theologies in a Time of Trump*, Boston University School of Theology, March 16, 2017).

76. Coloniality is "long-standing patterns of power that emerged a result of colonialism, but that define culture, labor, intersubjective relations, and knowledge production well beyond the strict limits of colonial administrations" (Nelson

Maldonado-Torres, "On the Coloniality of Being: Contributions to the Development of a Concept," *Cultural Studies* 21, no. 2/3 (March 2007): 243).

77. Shawn Copeland, "Political Theology as Interruptive," *CTSA Proceedings* 59 (November 2004): 73.

78. Copeland, "Political Theology as Interruptive," 80. Gustavo Gutiérrez sees witnessing as prophetic denunciation (*A Theology of Liberation*, 152).

79. Copeland, "Political Theology as Interruptive," 80–81.

80. Copeland, "Political Theology as Interruptive," 81.

81. Luis Rivera Pagán, *Diálogos y Polifonías: Perspectivas y Reseñas*, (San Juan, PR: Seminario Evangélico de Puerto Rico, 1999), 282.

82. See Femmy Irizarry Álvarez, "Religiosos de Diversas Denominaciones Abogan Por Una Asamblea Constitucional de Estatus," *Primera Hora*, December 20, 2018, accessed December 24, 2018, https://www.primerahora.com/noticias/puerto-rico/nota/religiososdediversasdenominacionesaboganporunaasambleaconstitucionaldeestatus-1317667/.

83. See Dorothee Söelle, *Political Theology* (Philadelphia: Fortress Press, 1974).

84. Carvalhaes, "Hasta Que Salga El Sol."

85. See Dorothee Söelle, *The Silent Cry: Mysticism and Resistance*, trans. Barbara Rumscheidt and Martin Rumscheidt (Minneapolis, MN: Fortress Press, 2001).

86. Jürgen Moltmann, *The Politics of Discipleship and Discipleship in Politics: Jurgen Moltmann Lectures in Dialogue with Mennonite Scholars*, ed. Willard M. Swartley (Eugene, OR: Wipf & Stock, 2006), 41.

87. Gutiérrez, *A Theology of Liberation*, 104.

88. The approach and terminology of decolonial and postcolonial are not used interchangeably, as they are two separate fields of study. A postcolonial theology of liberation differs from decolonized theology, for it acknowledges the difficulty or impossibility of removing the colonized aspect from theology. It dabbles with the fact of "this is where we are" which is why one needs both fields to assess Puerto Rico's coloniality.

89. "Our enemies are not that big, we are just on our knees."

90. In the immediate aftermath of María Teresa Delgado analyzed the film *West Side Story*, where stereotypes of Puerto Ricans are narrated through the vision, words and understandings of White playwrights ("Puerto Rico and Maria: Histories and Vulnerabilities in the Eye of the Storm," paper presented at the American Academy of Religion Annual Meeting, November, 2017).

91. Gayatri Chakravorty Spivak, "Can the Subaltern Speak?," in *The Post-Colonial Studies Reader*, ed. Bill Ashcroft, Gareth Griffiths, and Helen Tiffin, 2nd ed. (Abingdon, Oxford: Routledge, 2006), 28–37.

92. "To write in Spanish would only reveal a layer of my subaltern self that only stops being subaltern because my readers read Spanish."

93. Enrique D. Dussel, *Ethics of Liberation in the Age of Globalization and Exclusion* (Durham, NC: Duke University Press, 2013), 293.

94. Dussel, *Ethics of Liberation in the Age of Globalization and Exclusion*, 298–99.

95. Dussel, *Ethics of Liberation in the Age of Globalization and Exclusion*, 293.

96. Dussel, *Ethics of Liberation in the Age of Globalization and Exclusion*, 294.

97. Dussel, *Ethics of Liberation in the Age of Globalization and Exclusion*, 296.

98. Dussel, *Ethics of Liberation in the Age of Globalization and Exclusion*, 297.

99. Benita Parry, "Problems in Current Theories of Colonial Discourse," in *The Post-Colonial Studies Reader*, eds. Bill Ashcroft, Gareth Griffiths, and Helen Tiffin, 48.

100. See Mignolo, *Local Histories/Global Designs*.

101. Frantz Fanon, *The Wretched of the Earth*, trans. Constance Farrington (New York: Grove Press, 1965), 169.

102. See "The Pitfalls of Nationalism," in Fanon, *The Wretched of the Earth*.

103. See Carmen Nanko-Fernández, "Alternately Documented Theologies: Mapping Border, Exile and Diaspora," in *Religion and Politics in America's Borderlands*, ed. Sarah Azaransky and Orlando Espín (London: Lexington Books, 2013).

104. Nanko-Fernández, "Alternately Documented Theologies," 45.

105. Edward Said, "The Mind of Winter," *Harper's* 269, no. 1612 (1984): 54.

106. Édouard Glissant, *Poetics of Relation*, trans. Betsy Wing (Ann Harbor, MI: University of Michigan Press, 1997), 91.

107. Discussing her experience in the diaspora, Teresa Delgado writes, "The captivity of silence in the absence of story kept me in an exile of sorts, a wandering state with no place to call home, a place with no ground, no stories in which to root myself" (*A Puerto Rican Decolonial Theology*, 68).

108. See Delgado, *A Puerto Rican Decolonial Theology*, 92.

109. Ashcroft, Griffiths, and Tiffin, *The Post-Colonial Studies Reader*, 137.

110. Albert Memmi, *Retrato Del Colonizado*, trans. J. Davis (Buenos Aires, Argentina: Ediciones de la Flor, 1996), 125–28.

111. Jonathan Calvillo, "Latino Evangelical Moral Identities: Remaining Ethnic While Reconceptualizing the Past" (paper presented at the American Academy of Religion Annual Meeting, San Antonio, Texas, November 2016). See also Ricardo L. Franco, "Borderlands Spirituality: Practical Theology and Ministry in Three Latino Protestant Congregations" (DMin diss., Boston University, 2017.)

112. Ashcroft, Griffiths, and Tiffin, *The Post-Colonial Studies Reader*, 517–18.

113. He argues for hybridity as a corrosion of hegemony: see Vítor Westhelle, *After Heresy: Colonial Practices and Post-Colonial Theologies* (Eugene, OR: Wipf & Stock, 2010), xii–xiii.

114. Westhelle, *After Heresy*, xi–xvii, 153–58.

115. Mark Lewis Taylor, "Spirit and Liberation: Achieving Postcolonial Theology in the United States," in *Postcolonial Theologies: Divinity and Empire*, ed. Catherine Keller, Michael Nausner, and Mayra Rivera (St. Louis, MO: Chalice Press, 2004), 39–40.

116. Taylor, "Spirit and Liberation," 53–55.

117. Anne Joh Wonhee, "A Postcolonial Spectrality of the Cross," in *Postcolonial Theology*, ed. Hille Haker, Luiz Carlos Susin, and Eloi Messi Metogo (London: SCM Press, 2013), 42–50.

118. "I am me and my circumstances . . . " from José Ortega y Gasset, *Meditaciones del Quijote* (Madrid: Madrid Residencia de Estudiantes, 1914), 43–44.

119. Jorge L. Bardeguez, "La Teología de La Liberación: Una Declaración Personal," in *Fe Cristiana y Descolonización de Puerto Rico*, ed. Luis Rivera Pagán (San Juan, PR: Mesa de Diálogo Martin Luther King, Jr., 2013), 27–40.

120. See Juan Caraballo Resto, "Dios como estrategia política," *El Nuevo Día*, February 8, 2018, accessed December 28, 2018, https://www.elnuevodia.com/opinion/columnas/dioscomoestrategiapolitica-columna-2397039/.

121. "Maafa" means terrible occurrence; it is the commemoration of the African Holocaust on the middle passage.

122. Arce Martínez, *Teología En Revolución*.

123. I do not pretend to present a naïve and/or absolute understanding of void as always having a positive outcome. I reflect, at the same time, about our Latin American siblings who cross the desert in pursuit of their hopes and encounter death along the way.

124. Stephen Skrimshire, *Politics of Fear, Practices of Hope: Depoliticisation and Resistance in Time of Terror* (London: Continuum, 2008), 187.

125. Skrimshire, *Politics of Fear, Practices of Hope*, 186–87.

126. Bryan P. Stone, *Compassionate Ministry: Theological Foundations* (Maryknoll, NY: Orbis Books, 1996), 157.

127. Stone, *Compassionate Ministry*, 158–59.

128. Jon Sobrino, "The Economics of Ecclesia," 88–89.

129. Fluker, *The Ground Has Shifted*, 39.

130. "Arm (or clothe) yourself with courage."

131. "We have an entire generation that will continue to live in the illusion of supposed stability and still the issue of political status [in Puerto Rico] is not resolved" (Collaborator #12, confidential interview by Yara González-Justiniano, Puerto Rico, March-April, 2018).

132. Collaborators #4 and #7, confidential interview by Yara González-Justiniano, Puerto Rico, March-April, 2018.

133. "I felt as if in that moment we were being baptized in a new reality, which is not just a socioeconomic and political reality, but a spiritual reality also" (Collaborator #2, confidential interview by Yara González-Justiniano, Puerto Rico, March-April, 2018).

134. Juan Luis Segundo, *The Community Called Church* (Maryknoll, NY: Orbis Books, 1973), 135.

135. See Elsa Támez, *When the Horizons Close: Rereading Ecclesiastes* (Eugene, OR: Wipf & Stock, 2006).

136. Elena Loiziduo, "Dreams and the Political Subject," in *Vulnerability in Resistance*, ed. Judith Butler, Zeynep Gambetti, and Leticia Sabsay (Durham, NC: Duke University Press, 2016), 126.

137. Keri Day, *Religious Resistance to Neoliberalism: Womanist and Black Feminist Perspectives* (New York: Palgrave Macmillan, 2016), 162.

138. Day, *Religious Resistance to Neoliberalism*, 161.

CHAPTER FIVE

1. In order to complete the proposed study in a timely manner the scope of the ethnographic component of my project is limited in four ways. First, it focused only on a limited selection of Roman Catholic and Protestant churches and does not account for the religious plurality of non-Christian traditions in the Island of Puerto Rico. Hope might look different for people who do not articulate a Christian hope or a hope tied to any religious belief. Second, I acknowledge the situation of immigration to and diaspora in the United States but do not include this experience as part of my data collection. Third, due to difficult mobility and access on the island, especially in the aftermath of María, my ethnographic research was limited geographically to the northeast section of Puerto Rico. And fourth, the interviews were done in Spanish and their translation is limited to the particular quotations I needed in English for this book.

2. Delgado, *A Puerto Rican Decolonial Theology*, 21.

3. See Freire, *Pedagogy of Solidarity*, 21.

4. Marshall, *Though the Fig Tree Does Not Blossom*, 94.

5. Teresa Delgado, "'Dead in the Water . . . Again': Life, Liberty and the Pursuit of Happiness in the Twenty-First Century," in *Theological Perspectives for Life, Liberty and the Pursuit of Happiness: Public Intellectuals for the Twenty-First Century*, ed. Ada Maria Isasi-Diaz, Mary McClintock-Fulkerson, and Rosemary P. Carbine (New York: Palgrave Macmillan, 2013), 68.

6. Alves, *Tomorrow's Child*, 15.

7. See "What Is Modern Slavery?," U.S. Department of State, https://www.state.gov/j/tip/what/, and Julia O'Connell Davidson, "Troubling Freedom: Migration, Debt, and Modern Slavery," *Migration Studies* 1, no. 2 (July 1, 2013): 176–95.

8. "Utopia lies at the horizon. When I draw nearer by two steps, it retreats two steps. If I proceed ten steps forward, the horizon moves ten steps away. No matter how much I walk, I will never reach it. What, then, is the purpose of utopia? That is its purpose: walking" (Eduardo Galeano, *Las Palabras Andantes* [Buenos Aires, Argentina: Católogos, 2001], 230).

9. Alves, *Tomorrow's Child*, 114.

10. Jules Martínez, "Living the Winds of Disaster: The Church in a Suffering Zone" (paper presented at the American Academy of Religion Annual Meeting, Boston, MA, 2017).

11. Pierre Nora, "Reasons for the Current Upsurge in Memory," in *The Collective Memory Reader*, 437–39.

12. Nora, "Reasons for the Current Upsurge in Memory," 439–40.

13. Alves, *Tomorrow's Child*, 91–95.

14. See Luis Méndez Vázques, "El Miedo a la Independencia, ¿De Dónde Viene el Cuco?," *El Post Antillano*, October 27, 2016, accessed January 21, 2019, http://elpostantillano.net/pagina-0/historia/17997-2016-08-27-14-27-51.html, and Wilda Rodríguez, "Miedo a la libertad," *El Nuevo Día*, February 22, 2016, accessed January 21, 2019, https://www.elnuevodia.com/opinion/columnas/miedoalalibertad-columna-2164718/.

15. "The challenge of the evangelical churches and its theological thinkers [in Puerto Rico] is to promote, through their creative faculties, the cultivation, and evolution of the process [of unification and national identity] assuming it as a project from a Caribbean and Latin-American nationality more free and just." (Rivera Pagán, *Desafíos y Polifonías*, 284, translation mine).

16. Alves, *Tomorrow's Child*, 171–72.

17. "The faith experiences that will make the church go on will come from the people" (Collaborator #1, confidential interview by Yara González-Justiniano, Puerto Rico, March-April, 2018).

18. Leonardo Boff, *The Path to Hope: Fragments from a Theologian's Journey* (Maryknoll, NY: Orbis Books, 1993), 123.

Bibliography

Alinsky, Saul David. *Rules for Radicals: A Practical Primer for Realistic Radicals.* New York: Random House, 1971.
Alves, Rubem A. *A Theology of Human Hope.* St. Meinrad, IN: Abbey Press, 1972.
———. *The Poet, The Warrior, The Prophet.* London: SCM Press, 2002.
———. *Tomorrow's Child: Imagination, Creativity and the Birth of Culture.* Eugene, OR: Wipf and Stock, 2011.
Anzaldúa, Gloria. *Borderlands/La Frontera: The New Mestiza.* 3rd edition. San Francisco: Aunt Lute Books, 2007.
———. *Light in the Dark = Luz En Lo Oscuro: Rewriting Identity, Spirituality, Reality.* Durham, NC: Duke University Press, 2015.
Arce Martínez, Sergio. *Teología En Revolución.* Vol. 1. Matanzas, Cuba: Centro de Información y Estudio Augusto Cotto, 1975.
———. *¿Cómo Es Que Aún No Entendéis?: Antología de Textos Teológicos.* Vol. 1. La Habana, Cuba: Editorial Caminos, 2009.
Aristotle. *Categories.* Translated by E. M Edghill. Blacksburg, VA: Virginia Tech, 2001.
Ashcroft, Bill, Gareth Griffiths, and Helen Tiffin, eds. *The Post-Colonial Studies Reader.* 2nd edition. London: Routledge, 2006.
Ayala, César J., and Rafael Bernabe. *Puerto Rico En El Siglo Americano: Su Historia Desde 1898.* San Juan, PR: Ediciones Callejón, 2016.
Bardeguez, Jorge L. "La Teología de La Liberación: Una Declaración Personal." In *Fe Cristiana y Descolonización de Puerto Rico*, edited by Luis Rivera Pagán, 27–40. San Juan, PR: Mesa de Diálogo Martin Luther King, Jr., 2013.
Benjamin, Walter. "The Storyteller" and "Theses on the Philosophy of History." In Olick, Vinitzky-Seroussi, and Levy, *The Collective Memory Reader*, 99–103.
Berlant, Lauren Gail. *Cruel Optimism.* Durham, NC: Duke University Press, 2011.
Berman Santana, Déborah. *Kicking Off the Bootstraps: Enviroment, Development, and Community Power in Puerto Rico.* Tucson, AZ: University of Arizona Press, 1996.
———. "Puerto Rico's Operation Bootstrap: Colonial Roots of a Present Model for 'Third World Development.'" *Revista Geográfica*, no. 124 (January-December 1998): 87–16.

Bloch, Ernst. *The Principle of Hope*. Cambridge, MA: MIT Press, 1986.
Boff, Leonardo. *Ecclesiogenesis: The Base Communities Reinvent the Church*. Maryknoll, NY: Orbis Books, 1986.
———. *The Path to Hope: Fragments from a Theologian's Journey*. Maryknoll, NY: Orbis Books, 1993.
Bonilla, Yarimar. *Non-Sovereign Futures: French Caribbean Politics in the Wake of Disenchantment* Chicago, IL: The University of Chicago Press, 2015.
Butler, Judith, Zeynep Gambetti, and Leticia Sabsay. *Vulnerability in Resistance*. Durham, NC: Duke University Press, 2016.
Caputo, John D. *Hoping Against Hope: Confessions of a Postmodern Pilgrim*. Minneapolis, MN: Fortress Press, 2015.
Coleman, Monica A. *Making a Way Out of No Way: A Womanist Theology*. Minneapolis, MN: Fortress Press, 2008.
Conde-Frazier, Elizabeth. "Being the Gospel Together: The Marks of an Evangélica Ecclesiology." In *Latina Evangélicas: A Theological Survey from the Margins*, 90–107. Eugene, OR: Cascade Books, 2013.
Connerton, Paul. *How Societies Remember*. Cambridge: Cambridge University Press, 1989.
———. *The Spirit of Mourning: History, Memory and the Body*. Cambridge: Cambridge University Press, 2011.
Copeland, Shawn. "Political Theology as Interruptive." *CTSA Proceedings* 59 (November 2004): 71–82.
Cotté Morales, Alejandro, Magda Orfila Barreto, Doris Pizarro Claudio, Wilfredo Quiñones Sierra, Raquel Seda de Calderón, and Luz Vega Rodríguez. *Trabajo Comunitario y Descolonización*. San Juan, PR: Fundación Francisco Manrique Cabrera, 2012.
Cruz, Krenly. *Historia Del Avivamiento Del '33 de Los Discípulos de Cristo En Puerto Rico*. Bogotá, Colombia: Editorial Buena Semilla, 2003.
Day, Keri. *Religious Resistance to Neoliberalism: Womanist and Black Feminist Perspectives*. New York: Palgrave Macmillan, 2016.
De La Torre, Miguel A. *Embracing Hopelessness*. Minneapolis. MN: Fortress Press, 2017.
Delgado, Teresa. "Freedom Is Our Own: Towards a Puerto Rican Emancipation Theology." In *Creating Ourselves: African Americans and Hispanic Americans on Popular Culture and Religious Expression*, edited by Anthony Pinn and Benjamín Valentín, 138–172. Durham, NC: Duke University Press, 2009.
———. "'Dead in the Water . . . Again': Life, Liberty and the Pursuit of Happiness in the Twenty-First Century." In *Theological Perspectives for Life, Liberty and the Pursuit of Happiness: Public Intellectuals for the Twenty-First Century*, edited by Ada Maria Isasi-Diaz, Mary McClintock-Fulkerson, and Rosemary P. Carbine, 61–69. New York: Palgrave Macmillan, 2013.
———. *A Puerto Rican Decolonial Theology: Prophesy Freedom*. London: Palgrave Macmillan, 2017.
Díaz Quiñones, Arcadio. *La Memoria Rota*. San Juan, PR: Ediciones Huracán, 1996.

Doyle, Dominic. "A Future, Difficult, Yet Possible Good: Defining Christian Hope." In Lennan and Pineda-Madrid, *Hope: Promise, Possibility and Fulfillment*, 16–27.
Dussel, Enrique D. *Ethics of Liberation in the Age of Globalization and Exclusion.* Durham, NC: Duke University Press, 2013.
Espín, Orlando. *Idol and Grace: On Traditioning and Subversive Hope.* Maryknoll, NY:
Orbis Books, 2014.
Estrella, Arturo. Ventana a la Esperanza: Un Proyecto para Puerto Rico. San Juan, PR: Editores Publicaciones Puertorriqueñas. 1996.
Eyerman, Ron. "From The Past in the Present: Culture and the Transmission of Memory." In Olick, Vinitzky-Seroussi, and Levy, *The Collective Memory Reader*, 304–10.
Fanon, Frantz. *The Wretched of the Earth.* Translated by Constance Farrington. New York: Grove Press, 1965.
Fluker, Walter E. *The Ground Has Shifted: The Future of the Black Church in Post-Racial America.* New York: New York University Press, 2016.
Franco, Ricardo L. "Borderlands Spirituality: Practical Theology and Ministry in Three Latino Protestant Congregations." DMin diss., Boston University, 2017.
Freire, Paulo, Ana María Araújo Freire, and Walter Ferreira de Oliveira. *Pedagogy of Solidarity.* Walnut Creek, CA: Left Coast Press, 2014.
Galeano, Eduardo. *Las Palabras Andantes.* 5th ed. Buenos Aires, Argentina: Catálogos, 2001.
García, Gervasio L. *Desafío y Solidaridad: Breve Historia Del Movimiento Obrero Puertorriqueño.* Río Piedras, PR: Ediciones Huracán, 1997.
Glissant, Edouard. *Poetics of Relation.* Translated by Betsy Wing. Ann Harbor, MI: University of Michigan Press, 1997.
Goizueta, Roberto S. "Corpus Verum: Toward a Borderland Ecclesiology." In *Building Bridges, Doing Justice: Constructing a Latino/a Ecumenical Theology*, ed. Orlando O. Espín, 145–66. Maryknoll, NY: Orbis Books, 2009.
González, José Luis. *El País de Los Cuatro Pisos y Otros Ensayos.* Río Piedras, PR: Ediciones Huracán, 1985.
Griffith, Colleen M. "Christian Hope: A Grace and a Choice." In Lennan and Pineda-Madrid, *Hope: Promise, Possibility and Fulfillment*, 3–15.
Gutiérrez, Gustavo. *The Power of the Poor in History: Selected Writings.* Maryknoll, NY: Orbis Books, 1983.
———. *A Theology of Liberation: History, Politics, and Salvation.* 17th ed. Maryknoll, NY: Orbis Books, 1988.
———. *The God of Life.* Maryknoll, NY: Orbis Books, 1991.
Halbwachs, Maurice. *On Collective Memory.* Edited by Lewis A. Coser. Chicago: University of Chicago Press, 1992.
———. "From Collective Memory." In Olick, Vinitzky-Seroussi, and Levy, *The Collective Memory Reader*, 139–49.
Haslip-Viera, Gabriel. *Race, Identity and Indigenous Politics: Puerto Rican Neo Taínos in the Diaspora and the Island.* New York: Latino Studies Press, 2013.

Isasi-Díaz, Ada María. *Mujerista Theology: A Theology for the Twenty-First Century.* Maryknoll, NY: Orbis Books, 1996.

———. *En La Lucha/In the Struggle: Elaborating a Mujerista Theology.* Minneapolis, MN: Fortress Press, 2004.

Kundera, Milan. *The Book of Laughter and Forgetting.* New York: Harper Perennial Modern Classics, 1999.

Lane, Dermot A. *Keeping Hope Alive: Stirrings in Christian Theology.* New York: Paulist Press, 1996.

Laub, Dori. *Testimony: Crises of Witnessing in Literature, Psychoanalysis and History.* New York: Routledge, 1992.

Lee, Jung Young. *Marginality: The Key to Multicultural Theology.* Minneapolis, MN: Fortress Press, 1995.

Lennan, Richard, and Nancy Pineda-Madrid. *Hope: Promise, Possibility and Fulfillment.* New York: Paulist Press, 2013.

Loiziduo, Elena. "Dreams and the Political Subject." In *Vulnerability in Resistance*, edited by Judith Butler, Zeynep Gambetti, and Leticia Sabsay, 122–45. Durham, NC: Duke University Press, 2016.

Maldonado-Torres, Nelson. "On the Coloniality of Being: Contributions to the Development of a Concept." *Cultural Studies* 21, no. 2/3 (March 2007): 240–70.

Marsh, Charles, Peter Slade, and Sarah Azaransky. *Lived Theology: New Perspectives on Method, Style, and Pedagogy.* Oxford University Press, 2016.

Marshall, Ellen Ott. *Though the Fig Tree Does Not Blossom: Toward a Responsible Theology of Christian Hope.* Nashville, TN: Abingdon Press, 2006.

Melucci, Alberto. *Challenging Codes: Collective Action in the Information Age.* Cambridge: Cambridge University Press, 1996.

Memmi, Albert. *Retrato Del Colonizado.* Translated by J. Davis. Buenos Aires, Argentina: Ediciones de la Flor, 1996.

Mendoza García, Jorge. "Exordio a La Memoria Colectiva y El Olvido Social." *Athenea Digital* 8 (2005): 1–26.

Metz, Johann Baptist. *Faith in History and Society: Toward a Practical Fundamental Theology.* New York: Seabury Press, 1980.

Mignolo, Walter. *Local Histories/Global Designs: Coloniality, Subaltern Knowledges, and Border Thinking.* Princeton, NJ: Princeton University Press, 2000.

Moltmann, Jürgen. *Hope and Planning.* New York: Harper & Row, 1971.

———. *The Church in the Power of the Spirit: A Contribution to Messianic Ecclesiology.* Minneapolis, MN: Fortress Press, 1993.

———. *Theology of Hope: On the Ground and the Implications of a Christian Eschatology.* Minneapolis, MN: Fortress Press, 1993.

———. *The Politics of Discipleship and Discipleship in Politics: Jurgen Moltmann Lectures in Dialogue with Mennonite Scholars.* Edited by Willard M. Swartley. Eugene, OR: Wipf & Stock, 2006.

———. *The Living God and the Fullness of Life.* Louisville, KY: Westminster John Knox Press, 2015.

Nanko-Fernández, Carmen. "Alternately Documented Theologies: Mapping Border, Exile and Diaspora." In *Religion and Politics in America's Borderlands*, edited by Sarah Azaransky and Orlando Espín, 33–56. London: Lexington Books, 2013.
Nora, Pierre. "Between Memory and History: *Les Lieux de Mémoire*." *Representations* 26, no. 26 (1989): 7–24.
———. *Realms of Memory: Rethinking the French Past*. New York: Columbia University Press, 1996.
———. "Reasons for the Current Upsurge in Memory." In Olick, Vinitzky-Seroussi, and Levy, *The Collective Memory Reader*, 437–41.
O'Connell Davidson, Julia. "Troubling Freedom: Migration, Debt, and Modern Slavery." *Migration Studies* 1, no. 2 (July 1, 2013): 176–95.
Olick, Jeffrey K. "From Collective Memory: The Two Cultures." In Olick, Vinitzky-Seroussi, and Levy, *The Collective Memory Reader*, 225–28.
Olick, Jeffrey K., Vered Vinitzky-Seroussi, and Daniel Levy, eds. *The Collective Memory Reader*. New York: Oxford University Press, 2011.
Ortega y Gasset, José. *Meditaciones del Quijote*. Madrid: Madrid Residencia de Estudiantes, 1914.
Parker, Evelyn L. *Trouble Don't Last Always: Emancipatory Hope Among African American Adolescents*. Cleveland, OH: Pilgrim Press, 2003.
Parry, Benita. "Problems in Current Theories of Colonial Discourse." In *The Post-Colonial Studies Reader*, edited by Bill Ashcroft, Gareth Griffiths, and Helen Tiffin, 2nd ed., 44–50. Abingdon, Oxford: Routledge, 2006.
Patton, Michael Quinn. *Qualitative Research and Evaluation Methods*. Thousand Oaks, CA: Sage Publications, 2002.
Pérez Alvarez, Eliseo. *Abya Yala: Discursos Desde La América Des-Norteada*. Mexico City, Mexico: El Faro, 2010.
Pineda-Madrid, Nancy. "Hope and Salvation in the Shadow of Tragedy." In Lennan and Pineda-Madrid, *Hope: Promise, Possibility and Fulfillment*, 115–27.
Ricœur, Paul. *Memory, History, Forgetting*. Chicago: University of Chicago Press, 2004.
Riessman, Catherine Kohler. *Narrative Analysis*. Newbury Park, CA: Sage Publications, 1993.
Rivera, Mayra. *Poetics of the Flesh*. Durham, NC: Duke University Press. 2015.
Rivera Pagán, Luis. *Diálogos y Polifonías: Perspectivas y Reseñas*. San Juan, PR: Seminario Evangélico de Puerto Rico. 1999.
Robiou Lamarche, Sebastián. *Mitología y Religión de Los Taínos*. San Juan, PR: Editorial Punto y Coma, 2006.
Rodenborn, Steven Michael. *Hope in Action: Subversive Eschatology in the Theology of Edward Schillebeeckx and Johann Baptist Metz*. Minneapolis, MN: Fortress Press, 2014.
Rodriguez, Jeanette. "La Tierra Theologies' Contributions to Creation Theologies." In *In Our Own Voices: Latino/a Renditions of Theology*, edited by Benjamín Valentín, 21–40. Maryknoll, NY: Orbis Books, 2010.
Russell, Letty M. *Church in the Round: Feminist Interpretation of the Church*. Louisville, KY: Westminster John Knox Press, 1993.

Said, Edward. "The Mind of Winter." *Harper's* 269, no. 1612 (1984): 49–55.
Segundo, Juan Luis. *The Community Called Church*. Maryknoll, NY: Orbis Books, 1973.
———. *Liberation of Theology*. Maryknoll, NY: Orbis Books, 1976.
Silva Gotay, Samuel. "Desarrollo de La Dimensión Religiosa Del Nacionalismo En Puerto Rico: 1898–1989." *Estudios Interdisciplinarios de América Latina y El Caribe* 1, no. 1 (June 1990).
———. *Protestantismo y Política En Puerto Rico, 1898–1930: Hacia Una Historia Del Protestantismo Evangélico En Puerto Rico*. San Juan, PR: Editorial de la Universidad de Puerto Rico, 1998.
———. *La Iglesia Católica de Puerto Rico En El Procesos Político de Americanización (1898–1930)*. San Juan, PR: Publicaciones Gaviota, 2012.
Skrimshire, Stephen. *Politics of Fear, Practices of Hope: Depoliticisation and Resistance in Time of Terror*. London: Continuum, 2008.
Sobrino, Jon. "The Economics of the Poor." In *The True Church and the Poor*, 83–100. Maryknoll, NY: Orbis Books, 1984.
———. "The Economics of Ecclesia: A Poor Church Is a Church Rich in Compassion." In *New Visions for the Americas: Religious Engagement and Social Transformation*, 83–100. Minneapolis, MN: Fortress Press, 1993.
Söelle, Dorothee. *Political Theology*. Philadelphia: Fortress Press, 1974.
———. *The Silent Cry: Mysticism and Resistance*. Translated by Barbara Rumscheidt and Martin Rumscheidt. Minneapolis, MN: Fortress Press, 2001.
Spivak, Gayatri Chakravorty. "Can the Subaltern Speak?" In *The Post-Colonial Studies Reader*, edited by Bill Ashcroft, Gareth Griffiths, and Helen Tiffin, 2nd ed., 28–37. Abingdon, Oxford: Routledge, 2006.
Stone, Bryan P. *Compassionate Ministry: Theological Foundations*. Maryknoll, NY: Orbis Books, 1996.
Swinton, John, and Harriet Mowat. *Practical Theology and Qualitative Research*. London: SCM Press, 2016.
Támez, Elsa. *Bajo un Cielo Sin Estrellas: Lecturas y Meditaciones Bíblicas*. Costa Rica: Departamento Ecuménico de Investigación. 2004.
———. *When the Horizons Close: Rereading Ecclesiastes*. Eugene, OR: Wipf & Stock, 2006.
Taylor, Mark Lewis. "Spirit and Liberation: Achieving Postcolonial Theology in the United States." In *Postcolonial Theologies: Divinity and Empire*, edited by Catherine Keller, Michael Nausner, and Mayra Rivera. St. Louis, MOz: Chalice Press, 2004.
Tinker, George E. *Spirit and Resistance: Political Theology and American Indian Liberation*. Minneapolis, MN: Fortress Press, 2004.
Vélez, Roberto. "'Because History Does Not Allow Us . . . ': Collective Memory and the Articulation of Mobilization Narratives in the Antimilitary Movement of Vieques (1999–2003)." PhD diss., University of Albany, 2008.
Vivian, Bradford. *Public Forgetting: The Rhetoric and Politics of Beginning Again*. University Park, PA: Pennsylvania State University, 2010.

Weedon, Chris, and Glenn Jordan. "Collective Memory: Theory and Politics." *Social Semiotics* 22, no. 2 (2012): 143–53.
Westhelle, Vítor. *After Heresy: Colonial Practices and Post-Colonial Theologies.* Eugene, OR: Wipf & Stock Pub, 2010.
Winters, Joseph Richard. *Hope Draped in Black: Race, Melancholy, and the Agony of Progress.* Durham, NC: Duke University Press, 2016.
Wonhee, Anne Joh. "A Postcolonial Spectrality of the Cross." In *Postcolonial Theology*, edited by Hille Haker, Luiz Carlos Susin, and Eloi Messi Metogo, 42–50. London: SCM Press, 2013.
Zerubavel, Yael. "From Recovered Roots: Collective Memory and the Making of Israeli National Tradition." In Olick, Vitnitzky-Seroussi, and Levy, *The Collective Memory Reader*, 237–41.

Index

absence, 73, 105, 108
agency, 6, 9, 32, 45, 84, 91;
  creative, 82, 88;
  political, 68, 80
Alves, Rubem, 15–18, 27, 34–37, 52, 76–79, 109–14
Anzaldúa, Gloria, 38, 45, 57, 64, 75–77
apocalypse, 44;
  apocalyptic, 44–45

birth, 39, 82;
  birthing, 15, 34, 36, 144;
  rebirth, 15
Borikén, 2, 118n4

capitalism, 1, 52, 54, 102, 109;
  disaster, 5, 44, 110;
  neocapitalism, 52;
  plantation, 3, 119n17
Catholic Church, 7–9, 19, 29, 85;
  church, 14, 31, 33, 36, 43, 45–91;
  Christian, 29, 53, 65, 71, 110, 129n10;
  practices, 17, 37, 40, 103;
  Protestant, 7–8;
  Puerto Rican, 13, 16, 39, 44, 64, 77.
  See also ecclesial practices
citizenship, 3, 55, 64, 135n24

collaborator, 17, 45–47, 123n78
collective, 34, 64, 68;
  action, 52–53, 56, 114;
  liberation, 24, 45;
  movement, 13, 29, 44, 57, 76;
  responsibility, 55;
  work, 87, 108–9, 113
colonial history, 2, 7, 12, 29, 39–40, 57, 69, 74
colonialism, 1, 3, 17, 39, 53–54, 68, 8–83, 89;
  neo, 15, 52, 68, 87;
  post, 83, 88
coloniality of power, 1, 9, 55, 75, 136n42, 137n76
colonization, 74, 83, 87, 101;
  decolonization, 5, 55, 69, 77, 89, 101, 111
colonizer, 3, 74, 80, 86
commonwealth, 3–4
communion, 60–62, 66
communitarian, 14, 49, 65
community, 12, 14, 27–29, 39–40, 47, 52, 54, 55–66, 85, 89–91
conociemiento de base, 23
lo cotidiano, 23, 74–75
creation, 15, 36–37, 77–79, 82, 89, 113.
  See also flourishing
creative act, 27, 36–37, 126n31.

151

See also creative agency
creativity, 27, 77–78, 87, 89, 91
cuento, 67–69, 71–73, 85, 89, 92

death, 1, 15, 30, 32, 44–45,
    91–92, 140n123
Delgado, Teresa, 6, 74, 80, 102, 104,
    138n90, 139n107
despair, 22, 24–25, 27,
    30–33, 36, 91–92
desperation, 24–25
displacement, 13, 79, 85
dignified life, 1, 84, 105
disillusioned, 27

ecclesial practice, 29, 58, 62,
    109–10, 113
economic, 1–9, 18, 26, 32, 40, 50,
    54, 106–107;
        socio, 1–2, 13, 37, 39, 101
elastic. *See* elasticity
elasticity, 16, 32–33, 38, 68, 89, 91,
    103, 108, 123n82
epistemology, 75;
    epistemological lucha, 76
eschatology, 25, 30, 37, 39, 103
esperanza, 26, 28–29, 101, 115
esperar. *See* wait
evil, 1, 14–15, 19, 28, 32–34, 56, 58,
    60–64, 78, 90, 101, 114
exodus, 1, 24, 28, 31, 37, 40, 77, 78, 89

la facultad, 38, 74, 112–13
flourishing, 7, 14, 16, 19, 26–27, 32, 40;
    creation, 19, 47, 58–59, 109;
    economic, 4, 54;
    human, 29, 38, 43, 81;
    social, 40, 88, 114
forgetting, 68–78
future, 3–5, 15, 19, 30, 36, 64, 68–72

God, 7, 12, 22, 30–33, 41, 51, 59–61,
    63, 66, 77–78, 81
governance, 3, 39, 54

hope:
    awaits, 29, 109;
    axis model, 17, 104–*07*, 109;
    at the center, 16–18;
    Christian, 14–15, 23;
    communal, 14, 28, 91;
    cultivate, 33, 39, 108;
    decolonial, 89;
    enacting, 1, 14, 16, 29, 57, 63;
    eschatological, 16, 30, 62;
    false, 15, 23, 25;
    for, 19, 21, 31, 34, 47;
    hindering, 13–14, 22, 37, 79, 103;
    illusion, 24, 27, 33;
    in, 12, 14–15, 16, 32, 57, 63;
    liberative, 17, 40, 109;
    materialization of, 47;
    as ontological, 18, 21,
        30, 38, 108;
    as practice, 33, 39–40, 64, 110;
    practices of, 13–14, 16, 25, 36,
        45, 90, 114, 123n82;
    principles of, 22;
    sustainable, 15, 18, 22, 28, 58, 66,
        84, 102, 109;
    theology of, 14, 18, 25, 28
Holy Spirit, 39, 41, 48, 60, 62,
    64, 66, 114
hopelessness, 1, 9, 22, 28, 44, 101
hurricane:
    María, 11–12;
    Saint Ciprián, 39;
    San Ciriaco, 10;
    San Felipe, 18, 40, 48
hybridity, 85–87

identity:
    Christian, 36, 71, 86;
    cultural, 74, 86;
    national, 53, 69, 85–86;
    Puerto Rican, 8, 39, 85;
    social, 72
imaginary, 17, 25, 53, 65, 67,
    74, 105, 114

imagination, 13, 16, 18–19, 22, 28, 32, 35, 68, 108–11;
  power of, 21;
  public, 18;
  theological, 7
independence, 4, 8, 39, 53, 55, 82, 85, 89
indigenous, 2, 78–79, 87–88
individual, 25, 28–29, 30–36, 86
islander, 10, 12–13, 86, 112, 117n2, 118n3

lament, 24, 50, 77, 80–82
law:
  gag, 4;
  P.R.O.M.E.S.A., 9–10
liberation, 62, 76–78;
  in bodies, 79–80;
  political, 80–82;
  practice, 24, 109;
  in space, 79;
  in time, 78, 79
LGBTQIA, 46, 56

marginality, 59–62, 66
Marshall, Ellen Ott, 32–34, 38–39
material reality, 1, 63, 69, 102
materialize, 26, 115
memory, 17, 67–76, 80–81, 85, 92;
  broken, 75;
  collective, 69–74;
  false, 67, 74
mental health, 25
midwife, 15, 36
migration, 13, 47, 50, 79, 84–86
mnemonic, 57, 76
Moltmann, Jürgen, 25, 29–33, 39, 81
movement:
  collective, 44;
  social, 51–57;
  worker's, 53–54

natural resources, 35, 40, 48, 57, 79–80, 109;
  nature, 44, 59, 103, 115

operation bootstrap, 3–5
oppressed, 23, 27, 34, 35, 55, 58. 74, 77, 80–86, 88, 101, 108, 113
oppression, 108, 110–11
optimism, 26–27, 38, 101, 108;
  cruel, 26–27, 36
Organization, 15, 34–37, 107–08, 113, 115, 127n64

paradise, 57, 75
pessimism, 26, 27, 55
play, 36, 111–12
poder de convocatoria, 81, 113
postcolonial, 17–19, 64, 67, 82–89, 138n88
presentiment (hunch, sense), 36, 38
promise, 30, 32, 37, 39, 76, 89, 101, 103, 105–06, 108–09, 114
Protestantism, 7–9, 65
proyecto de país, 65–66, 69, 78, 82–3, 86, 102, 104, 110–14
pueblo, 10, 52, 57, 60, 63, 65, 115
Puerto Rican:
  diaspora, 12, 25, 45, 65, 84, 86, 112, 117, 139n107, 141n1;
  diasporicans, 12, 86;
  flag, 4, 91.
  See identity

recipe, 18, 102, 104, 108, 113, 115;
  for sustainable hope, 102
remembering, 60, 67–69, 72–73, 77, 82
resistance, 8, 24, 52, 54, 57, 67, 76, 81, 85, 91

slavery, 2, 109
solidarity, 24, 36, 54, 56, 59, 65, 90, 102–03, 108–09, 112–14, 123n81
statehood, 3, 9, 54, 82

tax, 5–6, 9, 13, 52, 118n3, 130n14
telos, 29, 35, 47, 64, 108–09
trust, 24, 26, 33, 37, 50, 63–66, 105, 108, 113–114

United Statesian, 7, 13, 86, 128n106
unsustainability, 3, 26–27

Vieques, 6, 51, 54, 76;
  paz para, 57
void, 28, 37, 77–78, 89, 91–92,
  105, 140n123

wait, 26, 29, 33, 63–64, 105,
  108–10, 115
witness, 29, 68–69, 76, 80–82,
  84, 138n78

About the Author

Yara González-Justiniano is Assistant Professor of Religion, Culture, and Psychology at Vanderbilt University. Born in Fajardo, Puerto Rico, this *cari-dura* attended the University of Puerto Rico and received a Bachelor of Arts with a major in audiovisual communications and double minors in modern languages and theater. She received an M.Div. and a PhD in Theological Studies with concentration in church and society from Boston University. Her educational journey of interdisciplinarity informs the ways in which she approaches theological studies.

www.ingramcontent.com/pod-product-compliance
Lightning Source LLC
Chambersburg PA
CBHW020125010526
44115CB00008B/972